# Seminar Leader's Manual

## LEARNING
## PSYCHOTHERAPY

*A Time-Efficient, Research-Based,
and Outcome-Measured
Psychotherapy Training Program*

## ADVANCE PRAISE FOR
### *LEARNING PSYCHOTHERAPY*

### SECOND EDITION

"Drs. Beitman and Yue have produced a brilliant second edition of *Learning Psychotherapy*. This textbook and its *Seminar Leader's Manual* are the best way of teaching the basics of psychotherapy that I have encountered in my thirty years in academic psychiatry. Residents in psychiatry love this method of learning. The intense intellectual discussions, laughter, and warmth promoted by using this book in a seminar format are a pleasure to behold. The powerful new modules on Listening and termination are incredibly insightful. The experimental module, Future-oriented Formulation, brings Drs. Beitman's and Yue's truly remarkable creative vision of teaching psychotherapy to the cutting edge. The first edition was great; the second edition is fantastic. I give this training program my highest recommendation."

— Jeffery C. Hutzler, M.D., Associate Professor of Psychiatry,
Cleveland Clinic Lerner College of Medicine

A NORTON PROFESSIONAL BOOK

# Seminar Leader's Manual

# LEARNING PSYCHOTHERAPY
## Second Edition

*A Time-Efficient, Research-Based, and Outcome-Measured Psychotherapy Training Program*

**BERNARD D. BEITMAN, M.D.**
and
**DONGMEI YUE, M.D.**

**W. W. Norton & Company**
*New York   London*

For information about permission to reproduce
selections from this book, write to
Permissions, W. W. Norton & Company, Inc.,
500 Fifth Avenue, New York, NY 10110

Production Manager: Leeann Graham
Manufacturing by Hamilton Printing


ISBN 0-393-70456-4 (pbk.)


W. W. Norton & Company, Inc., 500 Fifth Avenue, New York, N. Y. 10110
http://www.wwnorton.com

W. W. Norton & Company Ltd., Castle House, 75/76 Wells St., London W1T 3QT

1  3  5  7  9  0  8  6  4  2

# Contents

# Answers to Forms

# Additional Resources

Your training program may find it useful to purchase the following instructional videotapes. These video resources are referred to or are illustrative of the textual material in *Learning Psychotherapy, Second Edition.*

Bernard D. Beitman and Dongmei Yue (1999). *Learning Psychotherapy* [video]. New York: Norton. Order at 1-800-233-4830.

Leslie S. Greenberg (1994). *Process Experiential Psychotherapy* [videotape]. Psychotherapy Video Series I. Washington, DC: American Psychological Association. Order at 1-800-374-2721.

Florence W. Kaslow (1994). *Individual Therapy from a Family Systems Perspective* [videotape]. Psychotherapy Video Series I. Washington, DC: American Psychological Association. Order at 1-800-374-2721.

Alvin H. Perlmutter, Inc., and Toby Levine (producers) (1992). *Psychotherapies* [video]. *The World of Abnormal Psychology* (vol. 12). Washington, DC: Annenberg/CPB Educational. Order at 1-800-532-7637.

Jacqueline B. Persons (1994). *Cognitive-Behavior Therapy* [videotape]. Psychotherapy Video Series I. Washington, DC: American Psychological Association. Order at 1-800-374-2721.

Everett L. Shostrom (producer) (1966). *Client-Centered Therapy* (Carl Rogers) [video]. *Three Approaches to Psychotherapy* (vol. 1). Corona Del Mar, CA: Psychological and Educational Films. Order at 1-949-640-4029.

# Seminar Leader's Manual

# LEARNING PSYCHOTHERAPY

*A Time-Efficient, Research-Based, and Outcome-Measured Psychotherapy Training Program*

# Introduction

We are attempting to give our trainees a conceptual foundation, a model of psychotherapy, that will serve them well in their clinical work. This foundation is broad, and is based on common ideas, strategies, and techniques. In this program, trainees are encouraged to think psychotherapeutically, not only during formal psychotherapy, but when consulting with other professionals, doing case management, practicing pharmacotherapy, interacting with supervisors, and working in the emergency department.

## THE PRINCIPLES BEHIND THE TRAINING PROGRAM

Our approach is broad, not deep. It goes across schools rather than down into one or several. We think of this approach as a conceptual foundation that is stronger and wider than its depth. Trainees develop conceptual knowledge and learn to think about the basic skills of psychotherapy, but they do not practice specific techniques intensively. We do not extensively practice empathic reflections for example, but we demonstrate them and have trainees practice them. You might want to encourage more practice.

This seminar is analogous to the psychotherapeutic relationship, in that the seminar leader, rather than lecturing, facilitates personal growth in psychotherapeutic knowledge and self-understanding. Instead of passively reading and listening to lectures, trainees are asked to participate in the seminar and to complete homework assignments. Since elements of group process definitely become manifest in the seminar, it offers an exercise in group dynamics as well. Here-and-now reactions to each other and to the seminar leader can also be identified for discussion. The group leader should be comfortable with managing group process.

You may find that this format does not fit closely enough with your own concepts of psychotherapy, and you may wish to adjust it accordingly.

While the training program includes many technical requirements and is highly organized, you will still find considerable flexibility. The combination of structure and flexibility is intended to reflect the reality of psychotherapeutic practice, in which basic concepts are molded to fit the circumstances of the individual patient and the context of the patient's experiences, as well as the skill limits and strengths of the therapist. We encourage you to make decisions that you believe will improve the education of the trainees at your site when variations on our recommendations seem indicated to meet their individual learning needs. One trainer had only 15 sessions available in his curriculum for an introductory course. He planned to follow up with seminars focusing on individual schools and strategies, and selected the "intentions" section of Module 2 and the rating of the Rogers's tape from Module 3, because the normative data from other sites provided comparison rating for his group. He used only the introductory text and second session from Modules 4 and 5, because they provided a foundation for learning about strategies from a variety of schools. He also chose two sessions from Module 6 and 4, one from Module 7, including CCRT (Core Conflict Relationship Theme) training, Analysis of Your Reactions to Other People (Form 22), and Transcripts from Borderline Patients (Form 23), to supplement his personal interest in an interpersonal psychotherapy model. You may elect to create a similar individualized course from these materials to suit your local needs.

You may also choose from several ways of evaluating your program. We evaluate our own application of it from three different perspectives, including pre- and post-evaluation (trainees' third session and related forms), Counseling Self-Estimate Inventory (COSE), and Global Impressions of Trainee's Change (GITC). You may want to use all three of these evaluations, or just the COSE, choose your own evaluation method from updated research information, or elect not to do evaluations at all.

Competence in psychotherapy depends upon many factors, chief of which is to develop and maintain an effective working alliance. Without a working alliance, patterns cannot be established nor leverage obtained to help change them. We encourage you to join in our effort to establish a working alliance data base against which you will be able to compare each of your residents now and into the future.

We are collecting Working Alliance Inventories (WAIs) from residents' patients across the United States, gathered after the third or fourth session. These results will be pooled and normalized to define general norms and outliers. You will then be able to compare each resident and your resident group with national averages to see where they stand. This data will give you a relative measure of their competency in this key psychotherapeutic variable.[*]

## GUIDELINES FOR CONDUCTING THE SEMINARS

The seminars are at once didactic learning experiences and group process experiences. The didactic experience can be conceptualized as horizontal—the seminar leader should try to cover the entire content assigned to that day. The group process experience can be conceptualized as vertical—an in-depth exploration of the many possibilities the case or concept presents. As examples of a horizontal experience, consider the 12 cases of resistance assigned as homework following the last session of Module 6. Here the trainees are asked to emphasize the best answer to the questions while minimizing the multiple possibilities represented in the other answers. This exercise indirectly teaches the necessity of selecting only one response from among several reasonable alternatives. In contrast, some issues draw unique experiences from the group. In another example from the resistance module, trainees may find themselves fascinated with the problem of silent patients, perhaps because they have encountered them and been unable to respond effectively. Their individual experiences with uncommunicative patients can provide the group with many variations on an apparently simple theme.

[*] Please contact Nancy Bumby, Ph.D. (bumbyn@health.missouri.edu), for further information.

Therapists encourage patients to reflect on their own experiences. Similarly, you are directly and indirectly asking trainees to step back from their own thinking, feeling, and behavior while working with of these modules. What verbal response modes do they already use but have not yet learned to identify in the context of psychotherapy? What are they intending when they respond to a patient? How well is the working alliance developing from the patient's perspective, and from their own? What patterns of dysfunction are they able to see in their own lives, as well as in their patients? What change mechanisms have they and their families tried to use? What stops them from learning psychotherapy? What is the range of their "nonprofessional" responses to patients and colleagues? We are constantly challenging them to activate and develop their observing selves.

As you design your curriculum for the modules please keep in mind that the modules are not intended to be followed in the rigid manner they are presented. The rigidity is offered as solid grounding from which individual variations can and should be created. Good teaching and good psychotherapy rely on clear, well-defined guidelines and structures. And the teacher therapist must flexibly adapt to the needs of the students (patients). The teacher (therapist) accommodates to the strengths and needs of the trainee group (patient) within their socio-cultural context. In addition, the teacher (therapist) comes with unique strengths, experiences, and weaknesses to which the group (patient) must adapt. Identify your own strengths. Define what you want to teach, the ideas about which you are most passionate. Do you want your trainees to go on for psychoanalytic training or become certified in cognitive therapy? Do you want them to become highly sensitive psychopharmacologists? Do you want them to become teachers of psychotherapy integration? Are there certain diagnostic groups you know well and want them to know well?

In addition, try using different teaching methods from those prescribed in the modules. Several programs have fun with role playing. For example, the group leader hands out a brief case description to one of the residents, who is asked to play the patient. They may be doing Module 4 on inductive reasoning. Another resident plays the therapist and is asked to find the patterns. The group watches and comments. Psychotherapy comes alive in the present!

Other group leaders insist that the residents bring in a brief patient summary of their own to be presented right at the beginning of each session. You might call it a "Module Minute." The summary could relate directly to the module being taught or could be a problem related to another module. The value of this exercise is that it brings the ideas of the modules into the present difficulties with real patients now.

## SUPERVISION

Supervision of trainees in the standard one-to-one model has remained the standard teaching method in most training programs. Unfortunately, supervision tends to be unregulated, with training programs leaving the content and methods to each supervisor's discretion. Although supervision may be seen in some ways to reflect the psychotherapeutic process and its four stages, the clarification of supervision objectives continues to be an important task in any effective training program. In this introduction to our training program, let us briefly describe how the supervisory process parallels the didactic program.

An integrative supervisor should tailor the supervisory experience to the educational and interpersonal needs of each trainee. The trainee should be carefully engaged in the supervisory relationship, with particular attention to elements of the working alliance, transference and countertransference responses, and mutual likes and dislikes. The supervisor should carefully evaluate the trainee's strengths and weaknesses relative to the goals of training. These areas of strength and weakness can be clarified by asking the trainee to discuss cases with the supervisor. Transference reactions to the supervisor that may intrude upon the learning process, and countertransference reactions to patients should be exploited as valuable learning opportunities. Discussion should nevertheless not involve the supervisee's personal life. The measures of relationship strength used for patient-therapist interactions can be profitably applied to the supervisory relationship.

Supervisors using this training program should incorporate features of current and recently studied modules in each supervisory session. Verbal response modes and intentions, the objectives of the second module, can be easily integrated into discussions of audio- or videotapes. The strength of a working alliance can be assessed by asking the patient about concordance with the therapist on the three subgoals of the working alliance: task, bonds, and goals. Transcripts of the trainee's pre-module therapy sessions will provide opportunities to discuss verbal response modes, intentions, and the working alliance, as well as ideas from the subsequent modules. Supervision should be vertical, using trainee transcripts, as well as case vignettes from each of the modules.

Each supervisor could be asked to complete the Global Impressions of Trainee's Change (GITC). The GITC is modeled after the standard outcome measure of medication clinical trials. It is found following the Flow Chart.

## TRAINEE SELECTION

Some authors argue that certain therapist personality characteristics are prerequisites for training in psychotherapy (Dobson & Shaw, 1993; Garfield & Bergin, 1971; Garfield & Kurtz, 1976). Training may help an individual enhance and refine a quality like empathy, but it cannot supply elements of character and intellect that are not already present (Sakinofsky, 1979). This issue is critical, because research has established that therapists' personal qualities are highly correlated with measures of the helping alliance (Luborsky, McLellan, Woody, O'Brien, & Auerbach, 1985).

Dobson and Shaw (1993) pointed out that the ability to build sound therapeutic relationships is a clinical skill that is relatively immutable during training. They believe that good relationship-building ability should be a selection factor for prospective cognitive therapists rather than a training issue. Luborsky (1993) noted that more research is needed to determine whether relationship skills can be taught. Binder and Strupp (1993) reported that their training program in the psychodynamic and short-term therapy modalities was not successful in teaching relationship skills, particularly management of negative therapeutic reactions. Breunlin, Schwartz, and Krause (1989) found that, in training family therapists, 50% of the outcome variability was related to pre-existing factors (e.g., initial knowledge, personal family experiences like marriage and child-rearing, and prior experience in individual therapy).

Can trainees learn relationship skills? The answer to this crucial quesion depends on how relationship-building skills are defined. Training programs should be able to improve the ability to listen, to reflect feelings, thoughts, and experiences, and to communicate ideas more effectively. Training programs cannot teach compassion and empathy, however. It may well be true that life experiences like marriage and parenthood extend one's emotional capacity for empathy, compassion, and communication far more effectively than academic training programs.

## PERSONAL THERAPY

Research suggests that psychoanalytic and humanistic practitioners have more often had an exposure to personal therapy than eclectic practitioners. Cognitive and behavioral therapists appear to have had the least exposure to personal psychotherapy among adherents to any of the major theoretic orientations (Robertson, 1995). Robertson (1995) also concluded that those who have had personal therapy are more likely to view personal change as difficult and risky than are practitioners who have not undergone treatment; they are also more likely to believe that therapy strengthens self-awareness, self-nurturance, and self-disclosure. Perhaps, having been in the patient's role, these practitioners understand how valuable the therapeutic relationship is to the patient; they have experienced the vulnerability and susceptibility to influence inherent in that role. Whether personal therapy is a decisive factor in increasing therapeutic effectiveness has yet to be definitively determined.

## Flow Chart of the Training Sessions

|  | Seminar Leader | Homework |
|---|---|---|
| **Pretraining** | | |
| **Session 1** | Introduce the 8 modules of the training program, training methods, the goals of the training program. Be sure trainees complete COSE (Counseling Self-Estimate Inventory, Pretraining) within the session. Collect these forms after the session. | Each trainee is required to audiotape or videotape one psychotherapy session for about 20 minutes (will use this transcript in Module 2). Complete Working Alliance Inventory–Form T (by trainees) and Working Alliance Inventory–Form P (by patients) |
| **Module 1** | | |
| Trainees' sessions should be transcribed. The transcription will be used in Module 2. | | |
| **Session 1** | Review general introduction and introduction to Form 1. | Complete Form 1. View the 1–3 sessions from each of the 3 cases on the CD-ROM *Social Work Skills Demonstrated* and *Helping Skills* cases. |
| **Session 2** | Discuss answers to Form 1 with the group. Discuss the introduction to Form 2 with the group. Review questions regarding the sessions viewed on the CD-ROM *Social Work Skills Demonstrated.* | Complete Form 2. View the nonverbal behavior examples on the CD-ROM *Social Work Skills Demonstrated* and *Helping Skills* cases. |
| **Session 3** | Discuss answers to Form 2. Review the introduction to Form 3. Discuss any questions regarding the examples viewed on the CD-ROM *Social Work Skills Demonstrated.* | Complete Form 3. Read Chapter 3 in the text book *Social Work Skills Demonstrated* and complete basic listening skills exercises in the Workbook section of the text as well as *Helping Skills* cases. |
| **Session 4** | Discuss answers to Form 3. Review answers to basic listening skills exercises in Workbook section. | Prepare for role playing as described in Session 5. |
| **Session 5** | Role play of therapeutic interview. | (Optional) Read Chapter 4 in the text *Social Work Skills Demonstrated* and complete the Pitfalls exercises in the Workbook and *Helping Skills* cases. |
| **Session 6** | Complete GI (A Guided Inquiry, Post-Module 1a) and COSE (Post-Module 1b) and collect them after the session. Review homework from Pitfalls exercises. | Preview introduction to Module 2. |

(cont.)

| | **Module 2** | |
|---|---|---|
| | Complete Global Impressions of Trainee's Change (GITC) after Module 1. | |
| **Session 1** | Go through Module 2 introduction and teach verbal response modes (Form 4). | Complete Form 5. |
| **Session 2** | Discuss Form 5 with the group. | Complete Form 6. |
| **Session 3** | Discuss Form 6 with the group. | Read Form 7. |
| **Session 4** | Teach intentions (Form 7). | Complete Form 8. |
| **Session 5** | Discuss Form 8 with the group. Distribute the transcript extracts of trainees' psychotherapy session videotaped or audiotaped during Pretraining. | Rate group members' verbal response modes and intentions in transcript excerpts. |
| **Session 6** | Discuss the rating of their own verbal response modes and intentions. | X |
| **Session 7** | Have trainees complete GI (Post-Module 2a) and COSE (Post-Module 2b) during the session and collect them. Continue the discussion of trainees' verbal response modes and intentions. | Preview Module 3 introduction. |
| | **Module 3** | |
| | Complete GITC after Module 2. | |
| **Session 1** | Review the introduction to discuss working alliance. Distribute the videotape of Rogers's session with Gloria to each trainee if it has been purchased by your institution. If not, select another tape. Teach trainees how to rate working alliance after trainees watch vignette from Dr. Rogers's videotape | Watch Rogers's session and then use Form 9 to rate his working alliance. |
| **Session 2** | Discuss trainees' rating on Rogers's working alliance. Distribute the videotape of Beitman's session with MF to trainees. Collect Form 9 for rating Rogers's session and the tapes after the session. | Watch Beitman's session and use Form 9 to rate Beitman's working alliance with MF. |
| **Session 3** | Guide the discussion of Beitman's working alliance. Collect Form 9 for rating Beitman's session and tapes after the session. Do statistics of trainees' rating for Rogers's and Beitman's working alliances. | X |

| Session 4 | Distribute the results of statistics of working alliance.<br>Discuss trainees' rating of Rogers and Beitman. | Read Form 10–1, Form 10–2 and Form 10–3. |
|---|---|---|
| Session 5 | Have trainees complete GI (Post-Module 3a) and COSE (Post-Module 3b) during the session and collect them.<br>Discuss Form 10–1 and Form 10–2.<br>Perform Boundary Violation Role Play, Form 10–3. | Preview Module 4 introduction. |
| **Module 4**<br>Complete GITC after Module 3. | | |
| Session 1 | Go through the introduction to discuss inductive reasoning to define patterns.<br>Review the "cherry pie" introduction to Form 11–1 with the group. | Complete Form 11–1.<br>Read Appendix I. |
| Session 2 | Discuss Form 11–1. | Complete Form 12–1. |
| Session 3 | Discuss Form 12–1.<br>Discuss how to do the homework of Form 13. | Complete Form 13. |
| Session 4 | Discuss Form 13 with the group. | X |
| Session 5 | Bring Beitman's videotapes with MF and MC, or use tapes of your own faculty.<br>After watching the two tapes, discuss the patients' patterns with the group. | Complete Form 11–2. |
| Session 6 (optional) | Session 6 is optional depending on whether or not trainees want to see additional psychotherapy sessions conducted by therapists at your site. | X |
| Session 7 | Discuss Form 11–2 with the group. | Complete Form 12–2 and Form 12–3. |
| Session 8 | Have trainees complete GI (Post-Module 4a) and COSE (Post-Module 4b) during the session and collect them.<br>Discuss Form 12–2 and Form 12–3 with the group. | Preview module 5 introduction. |
| **Module 5**<br>Complete GITC after Module 4. | | |
| Session 1 | Go through the Module 5 introduction. | Read Module 5 introduction, Appendix II and III. |

(cont.)

| Session 2 | Continue to discuss the introduction. Demonstrate how to do Form 14–1. | Complete Form 14–1. |
|---|---|---|
| Session 3 | Discuss Form 14–1. | Complete Form 15–1. |
| Session 4 | Discuss Form 15–1. | X |
| Session 5 | Bring the videotape for Module 5. Guide the discussion after watching each videotape vignette. | X |
| Session 6 | Continue to watch videotapes and guide the discussion. | Complete Form 14–2. |
| Session 7 | Discuss Form 14–2. | Complete Form 15–2. |
| Session 8 | Have trainees complete GI (Post-Module 5a) and COSE (Post-Module 5b) in the session and collect them. Discuss Form 15–2. | Preview Module 6 introduction. |

**Module 6**

Completing GITC after Module 5.

| Session 1 | Go through the Module 6 introduction with the group. | Complete Form 16 |
|---|---|---|
| Session 2 | Discuss Form 16. | Complete Form 17. |
| Session 3 | Have trainees complete GI (Post-Module 6a) and COSE (Post-Module 6b) in the session and collect them. Discuss Form 17. | Preview Module 7 introduction. |

**Module 7**

Complete GITC after Module 6.

| Session 1 | Go through Module 7 introduction with the group. | Read Module 7 introduction |
|---|---|---|
| Session 2 | Continue to go through Module 7 introduction with the group. | Read Module 7 introduction. |
| Session 3 | Teach CCRT method. Go through Form 18. Teach how to use CCRT to rate transference (Form 19). | Complete Form 20. |
| Session 4 | Discuss Form 20. | Read Appendix IV and complete Form 21. |
| Session 5 | Discuss Appendix IV and Form 21. | X |

| Session 6 | Bring Beitman's videotapes with J and the videotape of Beitman's self-description of his reaction to the patient.<br>Watch videotapes and discuss transference and countertransference. | Complete Form 22. |
|---|---|---|
| Session 7 | Discuss Form 22. | Complete Form 23. |
| Session 8 | Discuss Form 23. | Complete Form 24. |
| Session 9 | Discuss Form 24. | Complete Form 25. |
| Session 10 | Have trainees complete GI (Post-Module 7a) and COSE (Post-Module 7b) during the session and collect them.<br>Discuss Form 25. | Preview introduction to Module 8 |
| **Module 8**<br>Completing GITC after Module 7. | | |
| Session 1 | Review the introduction to Module 8 with the group. | Read Module 8 text. |
| Session 2 | Continue to discuss the introduction. | Complete Form 26. |
| Session 3 | Discuss answers to Form 26. | Complete Form 27 (case vignettes 1–8). |
| Session 4 | Discuss answers to Form 26. | Complete Form 27 (case vignettes 1–8). |
| Session 5 | Discuss answers to Form 27. | (Optional) Complete Form 28. |
| Session 6 | Complete GI (Post-Module 8a) and COSE (Post-Module 8b).<br>Discuss answers to Form 28.<br>Provide feedback about the training modules. | X |

## Global Impressions of Trainee's Change

Trainee's Name_____          Rater_____

### *Baseline Evaluation*

### After Module 1 (Date_____ )

Given your experience with this psychotherapy trainee, how good a therapist is he/she?

①  ☐ Excellent           ④  ☐ Not good/not poor
②  ☐ Very good           ⑤  ☐ Poor
③  ☐ Good                ⑥  ☐ Very poor

### *Global Improvement After Each Module*

### After Module 2 (Date_____ )

1. Given your experience with this psychotherapy trainee, how good a therapist is he/she?

①  ☐ Excellent           ④  ☐ Not good/not poor
②  ☐ Very good           ⑤  ☐ Poor
③  ☐ Good                ⑥  ☐ Very poor

2. Compared with his/her ability at the end of Module 1 (baseline assessment), how much has he/she changed? Rate total improvement, whether or not it is due entirely to the psychotherapy training program.

①  ☐ Much improved        ⑤  ☐ Minimally worse
②  ☐ Moderately improved  ⑥  ☐ Moderately worse
③  ☐ Minimally improved   ⑦  ☐ Much worse
④  ☐ No change

### After Module 3 (Date_____ )

1. Given your experience with this psychotherapy trainee, how good a therapist is he/she?

①  ☐ Excellent           ④  ☐ Not good/not poor
②  ☐ Very good           ⑤  ☐ Poor
③  ☐ Good                ⑥  ☐ Very poor

2. Compared with his/her ability at the end of Module 1 (baseline assessment), how much has he/she changed? Rate total improvement, whether or not it is due entirely to the psychotherapy training program.

①  ☐ Much improved        ⑤  ☐ Minimally worse
②  ☐ Moderately improved  ⑥  ☐ Moderately worse
③  ☐ Minimally improved   ⑦  ☐ Much worse
④  ☐ No change

**After Module 4** (Date_____ )

1. Given your experience with this psychotherapy trainee, how good a therapist is he/she?

① ☐ Excellent      ④ ☐ Not good/not poor
② ☐ Very good      ⑤ ☐ Poor
③ ☐ Good      ⑥ ☐ Very poor

2. Compared with his/her ability at the end of Module 1 (baseline assessment), how much has he/she changed? Rate total improvement, whether or not it is due entirely to the psychotherapy training program.

① ☐ Much improved      ⑤ ☐ Minimally worse
② ☐ Moderately improved      ⑥ ☐ Moderately worse
③ ☐ Minimally improved      ⑦ ☐ Much worse
④ ☐ No change

**After Module 5** (Date_____ )

1. Given your experience with this psychotherapy trainee, how good a therapist is he/she?

① ☐ Excellent      ④ ☐ Not good/not poor
② ☐ Very good      ⑤ ☐ Poor
③ ☐ Good      ⑥ ☐ Very poor

2. Compared with his/her ability at the end of Module 1 (baseline assessment), how much has he/she changed? Rate total improvement, whether or not it is due entirely to the psychotherapy training program.

① ☐ Much improved      ⑤ ☐ Minimally worse
② ☐ Moderately improved      ⑥ ☐ Moderately worse
③ ☐ Minimally improved      ⑦ ☐ Much worse
④ ☐ No change

**After Module 6** (Date_____ )

1. Given your experience with this psychotherapy trainee, how good a therapist is he/she?

① ☐ Excellent      ④ ☐ Not good/not poor
② ☐ Very good      ⑤ ☐ Poor
③ ☐ Good      ⑥ ☐ Very poor

2. Compared with his/her ability at the end of Module 1 (baseline assessment), how much has he/she changed? Rate total improvement, whether or not it is due entirely to the psychotherapy training program.

① ☐ Much improved      ⑤ ☐ Minimally worse
② ☐ Moderately improved      ⑥ ☐ Moderately worse
③ ☐ Minimally improved      ⑦ ☐ Much worse
④ ☐ No change

**After Module 7** (Date_____ )

1. Given your experience with this psychotherapy trainee, how good a therapist is he/she?

① □ Excellent  ④ □ Not good/not poor
② □ Very Good  ⑤ □ Poor
③ □ Good  ⑥ □ Very Poor

2. Compared with his/her ability at the end of Module 1 (baseline assessment), how much has he/she changed? Rate total improvement, whether or not it is due entirely to the psychotherapy training program.

① □ Much improved  ⑤ □ Minimally worse
② □ Moderately improved  ⑥ □ Moderately worse
③ □ Minimally improved  ⑦ □ Much worse
④ □ No change

**After Module 8** (Date_____ )

1. Given your experience with this psychotherapy trainee, how good a therapist is he/she?

① □ Excellent  ④ □ Not good/not poor
② □ Very Good  ⑤ □ Poor
③ □ Good  ⑥ □ Very Poor

2. Compared with his/her ability at the end of Module 1 (baseline assessment), how much has he/she changed? Rate total improvement, whether or not it is due entirely to the psychotherapy training program.

① □ Much improved  ⑤ □ Minimally worse
② □ Moderately improved  ⑥ □ Moderately worse
③ □ Minimally improved  ⑦ □ Much worse
④ □ No change

# *Pretraining*

Pretraining has four purposes: 1) to introduce the modules to the trainees, 2) to have trainees complete the COSE (Counseling Self-Estimate Inventory, Pretraining), 3) to help each trainee obtain an audiotape of a minimum of 20 minutes of their own psychotherapy session, and 4) obtain a working alliance inventory from the audiotaped patient.

## Session 1

Review the general introduction to *Learning Psychotherapy, Second Edition,* focusing on the processes and goals of the training program. Trainees are asked to complete the COSE during the session. You should explain that the COSE will serve as a systematic self-evaluation through the entire program. Trainees are required to complete the COSE and the Guided Inquiry (GI) after each module. We recommend that a file be kept for these forms for each trainee. You will find useful observations in the GI about the seminar and individual responses to it.

The homework requires that each trainee obtain an audiotape or videotape of their own psychotherapy session. The session should be at least 20–30 minutes long. Right after this session, the trainee and patient each complete the Working Alliance Inventory. The trainee completes Form T (therapist's version), and the patient completes Form P (patient version).

The trainees are asked to transcribe their session so that it may be read by their colleagues for use in Module 2, Session 6. In this session, colleagues are asked to guess the verbal response modes and intentions behind each trainee response in each transcript.

The Working Alliance Inventories are to be scored by using the scoring methods described in the Leader's Manual of Module 3 on the Working Alliance. These data will be used in Module 3 to demonstrate similarities and differences in patient and therapist perceptions of the therapeutic relationship. The intent here is to encourage trainees to consider the value of data from standardized questionnaires in providing objective views of the psychotherapeutic process.

The Working Alliance forms are contained in the pretraining section of the Trainee's Manual. These are the 12-item forms of the Working Alliance Inventory.

### Common Audiotape Questions

Trainees had several questions in regard to these assignments.

"One of my friends is under a great deal of stress. May I use him as a patient?" Clearly, we recommend that only people with whom the trainees have had no previous relationship be defined as patients.

"I don't have any psychotherapy patient. What should I do to complete the Working Alliance Inventory?" Residents can find patients anywhere in their clinical experiences.

"Why should I do an audiotape when I know so little about psychotherapy?" We try to assure them that we are not trying to evaluate psychotherapy skills or knowledge, but rather to demonstrate some information about intentions and measuring the Working Alliance.

### Working Alliance Inventory Statistics

Statistics on the Working Alliance Inventory may be done by each trainee in a session or by the seminar leader. These results will be discussed in Module 3, Session 4. Each trainee's transcribed version will be used in Module 1, Session 6 to discuss verbal response modes and intentions.

# MODULE 1

# *Basic Listening Skills*

## SESSIONS

For the first session and for most of the other sessions of each module, the paragraphs are numbered as follows: Paragraph 1 contains instructions to you about how to conduct the session; Paragraph 2 contains experiences from our trainees; and Paragraph 3 describes the homework for the next session.

### Session 1

Purpose: Review the text of Module 1 in *Learning Psychotherapy, Second Edition,* and practice listening for what is not spoken.

**1.** Review general introduction and introduction to Form 1: Listening to What is Not Spoken.

**2.** Trainees sometimes had trouble with Freud's "evenly hovering" attention, but the term made them consider how attention can be modulated from overly intense, to intense, to neutral, to mildly intense, and finally to withdrawal and thinking about something else. The withdrawal to something else could reflect the therapist's own reaction to the patient, but could also be about what's for lunch or the therapist's attempts to keep awake. The idea of speech being incomplete was at once obvious and thought provoking. Asking them to notice when they cannot understand the patient's ideas fully, when something seems to be missing, became a hint to catching what was missing. Hidden meanings were not synonymous with the psychoanalytic term *latent content*. Latent content could only be identified through conversations about the ideas in question. Hidden content is a first approximation of what is not being said. Beyond this description, we were not sure how to distinguish them further.

**3.** Homework: Complete Form 1. The seminar leaders and trainees add examples from their own experiences of incomplete speech and hidden content. Optional: Trainees view the 3 sessions from the CD-ROM *Social Work Skills Demonstrated* (Sevel, Cummings, & Medrigal, 1999) or use related materials to train residents in the recognition of these behaviors. *Helping Skills* (Hill & O'Brien, 1999) may also be considered, especially Lab 2, Listening and Attending (pp. 96–98).

## Session 2

Purpose: Discuss unspoken, hidden meanings.

**1.** Discuss Form 1 and any questions regarding the sessions viewed on the CD-ROM *Social Work Skills Demonstrated* or similar video materials. The seminar leader may want to bring a copy of the video materials to class to do this more effectively. Review introduction to Form 2: Nonverbal Communication.

**2.** Trainees questioned whether the paranoid example was really an example of hidden content. Maybe paranoid people read too much into communication and look for hidden content where there is none. Trainees enjoyed the mother's reasoning for determining where the other son was. The question about how they listen provoked a great deal of discussion. Answering this question required the trainees to step back to activate their observing selves. Most people do not examine how they listen. They were amazed at the variety of ways people perform this basic human activity. Some listen for words; others prefer nonverbal communication; others just would rather not tune into others. For the most part, the trainees liked trying to figure out when speech was incomplete and how to ask about it. One trainee looked back at his internship experience and laughed as he read the vignette of the single mother with two children. An ER patient had made him feel quite strange and now he knew why—she was trying to get him into her life! The dream analysis was difficult for most of the trainees, but its purpose is to provoke some interest in their own dreams as well as those of their patients.

**3.** Homework: Complete Form 2. Optional: View the nonverbal behavior examples on the CD-ROM *Social Work Skills Demonstrated* or similar material.

## Session 3

Purpose: Study nonverbal behavior

**1.** Discuss Form 2 and any questions regarding the sessions viewed on the CD-ROM *Social Work Skills Demonstrated* or recorded sessions from other sources. Review the introduction to Form 3: Empathy and Summarizing. View video clip examples of attending behaviors during class. If using the *Social Work Skills Demonstrated* book and CD-ROM, note that Sevel and colleagues define *interpretation* somewhat differently that we do in Module 1. Because of this difference, leaders are asked to skip the interpretation skill examples on the CD. Leaders should click the "Behaviors in context" button, then "Example 1" to view the first example of the skill.

**2.** SOLER bothered several trainees. They thought they had to sit forward all the time! Others hated the idea of looking squarely into the eyes of the patient by sitting directly in front of them. We had not recommended either. Instead, it is suggested that trainees sit at angles which allow patient and therapist to look easily straight ahead with the option of looking directly at one another. This listening just for nonverbal behaviors challenged several trainees. Trainees were afraid that if they read the nonverbals too carefully, they might be considered dishonest.

**3.** Homework: Complete Form 3. Optional: Read Chapter 3 in the text *Social Work Skills Demonstrated,* and complete basic listening skills exercises in the Workbook section of the text. Or read Chapter 9, reflection of feeling, in *Helping Skills* and do exercises on pages 135–136.

## Session 4

Purpose: Discover the range of empathic abilities and expand your own personal range.

**1.** Discuss Form 3. Optional: Discuss basic listening skill exercises in the Workbook section of *Social Work Skills Demonstrated* or other related material. Try to help trainees to understand various forms of empathy (cognitive vs. emotional), as well as the difference between having an idea about what someone else is experiencing and saying something to them about it.

**2.** One trainee reported that he had been in another program where a board eligible anesthesiologist had switched to psychiatry. This ex-anesthesiologist was almost unable to listen and become empathic. The group thought maybe that was because anesthesiologists want their patients to feel nothing. Some trainees truly had difficulty with this exercise because they did not know how to tune into the emotional states of others. In moment of intense self-reflection and failure to monitor potential consequences, one trainee blurted out that she hated having to get into the experiences of others. Her mother had required her to sit and listen to her for hours while her brother and father did not listen at all. She wanted to do ER psychiatry. They wondered about the brain mechanisms of empathy. Did the amygdala play a role, or was it mirror cells in the insula?

**3.** Homework: Prepare for role playing as described in Session 5: Role Play of Therapeutic Interview.

## Session 5

Purpose: Actively learn to listen better, to read nonverbals and to convey empathy.

**1.** Role Play of Therapeutic Interview. The purpose of this role play exercise is to give trainees an opportunity to practice basic listening skills, including reflection of feeling, paraphrasing, clarification, and summarizing. In addition, they may practice basic attending behaviors, which include tone of voice, eye contact, body positioning, head movements, encouraging responses, and mirroring the patient's emotional/facial responses. First, trainees should form groups of three. Second, each person in the triad is assigned one of three roles: patient, therapist, or observer. Before the dialogue between patient and therapist begins, the trainee in the client role gives a brief summary of the problem situation she or he wants to explore. The problem situation should be sufficiently realistic and detailed for the patient to discuss it for several minutes. The therapist begins the dialogue by asking, "Given what you just told me, what would you like to focus on today?" The patient and therapist then carry on a "mini-session," in which the therapist helps the patient explore her or his issues. The dialogue should last five minutes; the observer keeps track of time. The observer also notes the therapist's use of SOLER techniques and other attending behaviors, as well as the role of nonverbal behaviors in helping the therapist to explore the patient's issues.

After the dialogue is finished, the trainee who played the patient gives feedback to the trainee who acted as the therapist about how effective she or he was in helping the patient explore the issues. The observer also gives feedback to the therapist. The trainee in the role of therapist should have the opportunity to respond to the feedback and include his/her own thoughts and feelings about the performance.

Next, trainees change roles, and the whole process is repeated until each participant has played every role.

**2.** As usual, residents are reluctant at first to actively engage, but moving seems to improve learning. Why? Perhaps the motor programs required to change during the learning process are more activated when the body is moving. Dividing up into groups of three has many advantages: a) trainees get to know each other better, b) more talking and observing can be done, and c) time is more efficiently used as a result. Some trainees are terrible actors but can play along once others show the way. Others get into roles very easily and enjoy having people pay attention to them. The observer role promotes excellent learning by forcing the trainee acting as the therapist to be more acutely aware of the person playing the patient. Because the observer is expecting empathic responses, adequate posture, and searches for hidden meanings, the person being observed will be more acutely focused on these important contents.

**3.** Homework (optional): Read Chapter 4 (Pitfalls) in the text *Social Work Skills Demonstrated* and complete the Pitfalls exercises in the Workbook.

## Session 6

Purpose: Module 1 encourages trainees to listen with both cognitive and emotional empathy. Seminar leaders should use their experience to help trainees focus on the mind of the other person—to be able to emotionally visualize the patient's current and past experiences.

Have trainees complete GI (Post-Module 1a[*]) and COSE (Post-Module 1b[**]) and collect them. Review homework from Pitfalls exercises.

---

[*] *Guided Inquiry (GI).* After extensive discussion and role playing, Heppner, Rosenberg, and Hedgespeth (1992) developed a semi-structured, open-ended questionnaire called the GI to assess how clients specifically construct and interpret the change process and counselor's behavior over time. It was hoped that data reflecting patients' phenomenological construction of therapeutic events would provide important information about how patients find meaning in major events within counseling. The results of the initial research (Heppner et al., 1992) revealed that the Guided Inquiry provided a rich source of information about patients' construction of the change process in counseling, and seemed to add another dimension to understanding the change process. Later research has found the Guided Inquiry to be useful in understanding students' experiences in multicultural training (Heppner & O'Brien, 1997), as well as later qualitative studies of the counseling process (Heppner & Mintz, 1997).

[**] *Counseling Self-Estimate Inventory (COSE).* The COSE operationalizes counseling self-efficacy, defined as one's beliefs or judgments about one's abilities to effectively counsel a patient in the near future (Larson & Daniels, 1998). The COSE measures one's self-estimate of future performance; it does not measure counseling performance. It has been shown to relate moderately to counseling performance (Larson, Suzuki, Gillespie, Potenza, Toulouse, & Bechtel, 1992; White, 1996). Scores can range from 37 to 222, with higher scores indicating greater counseling self-efficacy. Larson and colleagues (1992) reported that the internal consistency was 93 and the three-week test-retest reliability was 87. Validity estimates for the COSE indicate that (a) the COSE and anxiety significantly predicted counselor performance, (b) trainees' COSE scores increased about one standard deviation over practicum, (c) counselors and psychologists reported higher COSE scores than prepracticum trainees, (d) people with at least one semester of supervision report higher COSE scores than people with no supervision, (e) the COSE was positively related to self-esteem, self-evaluation, positive affect, and outcome expectations (Daniels, 1997; Larson et al., 1992; Larson, Cardwell, & Majors, 1996), (f) the COSE was negatively related to anxiety and negative affect (Alvarez, 1995; Daniels, 1997; De Graaf, 1996; Larson et al., 1996; Larson et al., 1992), and (g) the COSE minimally correlated with defensiveness, aptitude, achievement, age, personality type, and time spent as a client, and did not appear to differ across gender or theoretical orientation (Alvarez, 1995; Larson et al., 1992). Larson and Daniels (1998) provided an integrative review of the literature that examined counseling self-efficacy. Larson (1998a, 1998b) described how-counseling self-efficacy was embedded in social cognitive theory as presented by Bandura (e.g., 1986), and how self-efficacy is one construct in a larger theory to explain how counselors and therapists learn to become effective with clients.

# ANSWERS TO FORM 1

## Listening to What is Not Spoken

1. The question, "How do you listen?" provoked a variety of responses. Apparently people listen in many different ways. Several emphasized how context influenced how they listened: e.g., Listening to friends versus family members versus patients; listening early in the therapeutic relationship or early in the process of problem definition. Is there a characteristic way people listen across situations? Some of the ways people reported that they listened in our groups include:

   a. "I don't listen much. I just react."

   b. "Sometimes I think my own thoughts and then realize that I had not been listening to the other person. I wonder what I missed and whether I should ask about it."

   c. "I listen for the key ideas the person is trying to convey to me. I also listen for other peripheral information that might be of use to me."

   d. "As I listen, I think about what I can do to change the situation. My children call that manipulative."

   e. "People play in a limited number of human dramas. I try to match what the person is telling me with one of the many possible dramas. I do that with my wife as well as professionally."

   f. "I listen for how connected or disconnected to other people they are. I wonder whether or not they truly want me to listen."

   g. "I ask when, how, what, who questions in order to run a video in my mind of what they are describing. I try to get them to give me a solution to their problem. I monitor my relationship with them, trying to establish rapport."

   h. "I look for things that are unusual, out of the ordinary. I ask, 'what do you expect from me?' I formulate what I want to give."

   i. "I move in and out of listening. I do much self-monitoring. My internal reactions are valuable guides, especially for incongruent things. I clarify the meaning and intent of the other person."

   j. "I listen to the music and not the words. I search for connections, how they structure relationships."

   k. "I try to understand the context from which the person is coming."

   l. "I am afraid of being a sponge. I listen too much. I get too absorbed in what the other person is saying and cannot get to problem solving very well."

   m. "I stay focused. How much time do I have now and into the future? If I have a long time, I let the process flow. If the time is short, I listen more intensely. I struggle with deciding when to listen openly and when to cluster the problem into a diagnosis. Also the intensity of the problem helps to determine how I listen."

   n. "I try to get into their space. I pay attention to their breathing and other body rhythms like tapping their feet."

2. a. What is going on that is making you feel this way?

   b. How did he hurt your feelings?

   c. What happened that made you feel out of place?

3. If the therapist is a man: "I want you to be interested in me."
   If the therapist is a woman: "In order for me to be successful, I need a man in my life. I am inadequate for dealing with my life."

4. a) His implicit message might have been, "How can you be having a good time with me?" or "Please tell me it is me you are enjoying."

   One group was divided evenly among the men and women. The men knew he was asking for reassurance. Some men in other groups did not see the possibility that he might be looking for a compliment from her. They thought he was distracted, not paying attention to her. The women (in this and other groups) knew she would react negatively to what he said because it diminished the importance she was giving to the occasion.

   b) She reacted by being angry and hurt. Why? Because his response seemed to suggest the only good thing was the coffee when she was trying to say how much she enjoyed their time together.

5. J., you talked too much.

6. She may be afraid that the therapist will force her to take something she does not like. She may be bringing up the dream because the therapist has already threatened her with something he has said or done. Perhaps she would be willing to talk about it. In regard to other people in her life, she may be caught in a relationship which is both bad and good for her, but which the real world says she should end.

## ANSWERS TO FORM 2

### Nonverbal Communication

1. He is angry and hurt by her behavior.
2. Her family might not be as normal as she would like to think.
3. Therapist is likely to feel incompetent and/or angry. The patient may easily accuse others as well of not being competent or effective.

## ANSWERS TO FORM 3

### Empathy and Summarizing

1. You feel angry because she does not let you express your feelings while over-stating her own problems.
2. You feel unhappy because he did not appreciate the effort you went through for him.
3. You and your parents are in conflict because you have different goals for your college education.
4. It sounds like you and your sister have some conflicts regarding how much you should be involved in her life.

# Verbal Response Modes and Intentions

## SESSIONS

### Session 1

Purpose: To review the text of Module 2 in *Learning Psychotherapy, Second Edition,* and review the verbal response modes. Verbal response modes reflect communication patterns of the therapist that are pantheoretical and fundamental to all schools of psychotherapy. We teach verbal response modes to broaden trainees' communication styles by learning new response categories and becoming increasingly aware of verbal response modes they already use but have not recognized in the context of psychotherapy.

**1.** You discuss the definitions of each of the verbal response modes (Form 4) with the group. You can ask one trainee to read the definition and comment, and then ask others to comment. Trainees will disagree on several verbal response modes. These disagreements are critical to the learning process, since resolution requires careful consideration of the elements of each mode. You should help them to clarify, distinguish, and compare any verbal response modes that they have trouble understanding.

**2.** Some have trouble discriminating between *reflections* and *restatements, interpretations* and *confrontations*. They are likely to apply their own definitions if they do not read our definitions carefully. You may help them to clarify by emphasizing the following: Reflection is defined primarily by its attention to *emotion;* restatement is essentially a repetition of what the patient has said; interpretation extends beyond what the patient consciously recognizes to establish a connection between isolated statements and events; confrontation is characterized by its two parts, the first of which is usually a statement, and the second of which usually begins with the word *but*.

Our trainees report that the verbal response mode categories help them to recognize responses they have already being making. Some realize that all they have been doing is gathering information by asking questions.

**3.** Homework: Trainees are asked to complete Form 5, the object of which is to categorize the verbal response modes used in one of Dr. Beitman's therapy sessions.

## Session 2

Purpose: To review trainees' ratings of Form 5. The discussion is intended to broaden the range of their response modes by forcing them to discriminate among and between complex response modes, especially restatement, reflection, interpretation, and confrontation.

**1.** Trainees are asked to read aloud each of the therapist's verbal response units and then to report and justify their ratings. Disagreements often reflect trainees' difficulty in understanding the response modes; discussion further clarifies the definitions. The ratings supplied by the authors (Answers to Form 5) serve as reference points that can help you to facilitate the discussion. Keep in mind that some of the "answers" may not be absolutely correct. The struggle to comprehend through dialogue provides the best learning experience. During the discussion, you should ask trainees to go back to the actual definitions in Form 4, especially when the comments begin to wander.

**2.** Again, misunderstandings and disagreements often occur between restatement and reflection, interpretation and confrontation, and open and closed questions. Our own trainees have often struggled with the phrase, "So this week you got in touch with your anger." Is this a restatement or reflection? While studying the comment, "it was my impression last time that you were skating on top of it but never or rarely visiting it", from the sixth therapist speaking turn, trainees have struggled to distinguish interpretation from reflection. These and subsequent discussions lead to a focus on feelings and a new understanding of the concept of interpretation as causal and somewhat beyond the patient's current awareness. The struggle to understand through discussion seems to advance understanding in a way that cannot be achieved by didactic presentation alone.

**3.** Homework: Trainees complete Hill's Sample Transcript Form 6 for rating verbal response modes.

## Session 3

Purpose: to discuss trainees' rating of Form 6. The exercise of Form 6 is the same as Form 5.

**1.** The procedure of this session is similar to the previous one.

**2.** Trainees generally find it easier to identify the Hill verbal response modes than those used in the Beitman transcript of the previous session. Discussion centers around some lingering disagreements in distinguishing modes. For example, is CO (counselor statement) "I hear you saying that you would feel freer to live your own life if you weren't living at home" a restatement, reflection, or interpretation?

**3.** Homework: Trainees review Form 7 (definitions of therapist intentions).

## Session 4

Purpose: To review Form 7. Intentions describe the therapist's objectives for each intervention. The study of one's intentions activates the observing self. Teaching intentions can improve trainees' ability to ask, "What do I want to accomplish?", at any given moment within the session.

**1.** The group discusses each intention one by one. Encourage trainees to comment on each intention, and help them to distinguish among intentions that can be easily confused, including *change, challenge,* and *reinforce change; support* and *catharsis; focus* and *clarify,* and so on. Help the trainees distinguish between the verbal response modes and the intentions, and understand the relationship between them. Various response modes can be used to accomplish the same intentions; for instance, the therapist could help the patient explore feelings and behaviors using an *open question, interpretation,* *restatement,* or *confrontation*. On the other hand, each response mode can be used to achieve several different intentions; for example, open questions can be used with the following intentions: *get information, cognition, feelings, catharsis,* and *relationship*.

**2.** This list of twenty definitions provides an outline of the techniques of psychotherapy. Examples like, *set limits* usually prompts discussion of the therapeutic contract and the handling of telephone calls with borderline patients. *Focus* helps to distinguish a naive, untrained listener from a more directing interviewer. *Cognitions* leads to a discussion of cognitive therapy, and more generally to the overarching influence of one's worldview on interaction. *Self-control* initiates discussion of responsibility and the recognition that therapists can only influence the patient in the office; the patient must be responsible for change outside the therapeutic session. We have added *interpersonal* to the list, because we believe it has discursive value as an individual category rather than as an adjunct or sub-set of the behavior category in which it was originally conceptualized.

**3.** Homework: Trainees complete Form 8, which is the same transcript contained in Form 7. This time, though, the trainees rate intentions rather than verbal response modes.

## Session 5

Purpose: To review Form 8. It is excerpted from Dr. Beitman's session with a patient. This videotape is to be shown in module 3. It is best for each site to develop its own tape and transcript, since intentions are best discussed with the person with whom they originate—the seminar leader.

**1.** Trainees are asked to report and justify their ratings. You report the intentions reported by Dr. Beitman (Answers to Form 8).

**2.** The trainees often wrestle with defining the primary intention of each therapist's speaking turn, as well as with some of the terms. For example, *focus* resembles *clarify*. You can ask the group to reread the definition and use diagrams or visual images to suggest that *clarify* means sharpening the current field of discussion, while *focus* means shifting to another field of discussion.

Trainees appear to learn from the struggle to understand and discriminate more clearly among various intentions, like: *feeling* and *cathart, cognition* or *behavior* and *insight, behavior* and *reinforce change, resistance* and *challenge. Insight* is particularly problematic, because trainees have had little experience with psychodynamic interpretations. We have described it as "making connections between the past and present," and then left it for discussion in future modules. Our trainees are asked to consider "cognition, feeling, and behavior" as part of defining patterns, not part of change. While *support* is an element of *reinforce change, reinforce change* is more specific. Trainees are encouraged to generate many answers and then to explain their answers to their colleagues. In this way, they begin learning the building blocks of psychotherapeutic intent.

This exercise has proven to be like a Rorschach test, as trainees differ in the primary intentions they perceive.

We prefer to use two sessions for this assignment because trainees need time to think about the purposes of their interventions. Again, right answers are less important than clarifying, focusing, and understanding the potential range of intentions.

**3.** Homework: Distribute extracts (about 1–2 pages) from trainees' transcripts of a pretraining relationship. Trainees rate the verbal response modes and intentions from each of these excerpts, skipping their own.

### Session 6

Purpose: To review selected exchanges from trainees' transcripts for verbal response modes and intentions. This exercise clarifies the goal of this module by giving each trainee the opportunity to consider what others think of his/her verbal response modes and intentions. Each trainee must then explain and justify his/her responses.

**1.** Trainees are asked to select one or two lines from their own dialogues. Other trainees then say what they think the verbal response modes and intentions are. Then the trainee-therapist explains his/her own answer. The trainees discuss the differences between their ratings and the therapist's. This comparison with the interpretations of others can help trainees gain further understanding of their own therapeutic intentions.

**2.** There is no need for you to define a "right" answer, since the therapist is present to explain his/her intentions. Trainees tend to answer in their own patterns, some seeing support, others seeing insight, and still others seeing change or reinforcing change.

Our trainees find this to be the most useful part of the module, since they can (1) see how others see them, (2) see how others do therapy, and (3) hear the intention directly from the therapist in the room with them.

### Session 7

Purpose: To complete guided questions (GI Post-Module 2a) and COSE (Post-Module 2b) (the first 20 minutes), to continue the discussion of trainees' verbal response modes and intentions (the next 40 minutes). After the session, you complete GITC (Global Impressions of Trainee's Change).

Once again, each resident selects a therapist turn. The other group members share their opinions of verbal response modes and intentions, concluding with the therapist's description and explanation of his/her intentions.

For homework, trainees should preview the Module 3 text in *Learning Psychotherapy, Second Edition.*

# ANSWERS TO FORM 5

## Transcripts of Dr. Beitman's Session
## (Rating Verbal Response Modes)

Each response unit is demarcated with a slash. The numbers immediately to the left of the transcript represent the averaged assessments of experienced & professional therapists about the appropriate category for each response unit. Numbers by the far left column are keyed to the following categories: 1 = minimal encouragement, 2 = silence, 3 = approval-reassurance, 4 = information, 5 = direct guidance, 6 = closed question, 7 = open question, 8 = restatement, 9 = reflection, 10 = interpretation, 11 = confrontation, 12 = nonverbal referent, 13 = self-disclosure, 14 = other.

| | |
|---|---|
| 4, 6 | **T:** I gave you a homework assignment last time. /How many pages do we have here?/ <br> **P:** Oh, probably 50. |
| 8, 6, 6 | **T:** Probably 50./And the homework assignment was to?/ What was the homework assignment?/ <br> **P:** Oh, about anger. |
| 7 | **T:** What about anger?/ <br> **P:** Describe my feelings about anger. |
| 8, 7 | **T:** Your feelings about anger./And, what happened?/ <br> **P:** As I began writing, I just went ohoooooo, and all these things from my childhood popped out, and I got in touch with my anger. (*laughs*) |
| 8 | **T:** (*laughs*) You got in touch with your anger./ <br> **P:** Yeah, I got in touch with my anger. |
| 9, 8, 7 | **T:** It was my impression last time that you were skating on top of it but never or rarely visiting it. /So this week you got in touch with your anger. /What was that like for you?/ <br> **P:** Well, at first when I was keeping the anger log, I was surprised, but then as I watched my pattern I noticed anger would arise and immediately I would squash it. (*coughs*) And so, I think it was Thursday when my mother was doing a number on me at the hospital, and I just said that's enough. And so, (*coughs*) |
| 6 | **T:** Do you want some water?/ <br> **P:** Yeah, maybe it would be good. I'm sorry. And ah, then I called both my sisters and I said that I was going to take a day or two off from going to the hospital. (*cough, cough*) Mother, she is ill, she is dying, but I never failed to do anything she asked me to do, but she begins demanding (pounds fist on chair), throwing fits like a three year old, you know, and "You, give me that," and I thought she wanted her tissues so I handed her the |

tissues. "No, no," but she wanted the lid that went on the hotplate. And so, when I gave her the tissues she threw it and "no, no, no" she says, and she is still pointing.

1

T: All right./

P: So I stood up to her. I put the tissues back on the tray and I said, "Well, damn, Mother, don't wait a minute, that'd be awful." And she looked at me like "what's going on here?"

8, 9, 8, 7

T: So you told your mother to cool it./ And that's a new experience for you. A relatively new experience for you. / So you at that moment decided not to go after what she was asking you to do. / Now, I'm curious about what that felt like for you too. /

P: Well, at the time I was just angry. I wasn't into evaluating myself. I was just angry.

8

T: Just angry./

P: At that moment, I decided I was doing part of this homework assignment, that I had a right to anger as much as anyone else. If other people are angry, I make excuses for them. They're tired, sick, or something. And then I realized, well how many of them make excuses for you? How many are willing to say, "Oh, you're angry."

6

T: If you express some kind of irritation? /

P: Um hmm. (*yes*)

8

T: You wrote in your diary that when you were growing up you were not permitted to have anger./

P: The messages to me in my childhood were that I had no right to my feelings. One time, I was lying on the bed crying, and my mother said, "What's the matter with you?" And I said, "I'm just so lonely." And she said, "Oh, hell you can't be lonely, you're with kids at school all day."

8

T: So she rejected your feelings./

P: Right.

8

T: She said your feelings don't count./

P: I grew up feeling ugly, dumb, lazy, because I couldn't be tired because children don't get tired. I was just lazy. I always figured my father was my buddy because he would sit down and talk to me. But what my father did was philosophize. If I was angry I should understand this person and well, you know, he had a bad marriage, or he was hurt in an accident...

10

T: So, your father gave you a model for how to make excuses for other people's feelings and bad behavior, and then you started being able to apply that way of thinking to yourself./

P: Um hmm. (*yes*)

8, 7

T: You've had more feelings in yourself this week than you have for quite a while,/ what's that been like for you?/

P: Well, after I stayed up all Friday night writing this, I began to see these patterns and realized that a child comes into the world as a clean slate and then people start writing on it. And so many of these beliefs that had been pounded into my head were not my beliefs. I felt like there was a chance for me to be free of them to think my own thoughts. It felt great!

8, 9      T: You seem to describe feeling liberated from other people's imposed rules and attitudes on you,/ and that was a very wonderful feeling for you./

P: Um hmm. (*yes*)

\*\*\*

10, 5, 13      T: And, now you're entering a phase where you're going to be able to express anger differently from before./ Maybe you will need to be able to say something like, "I'm angry," to somebody. Or, "What you said has made me feel angry." / I keep trying to find ways to label your feelings, but I have difficulty./

P: (*coughs*) I'm slippery (*laughs*).

8, 8, 13, 3      T: You're slippery./ Yeah, there are feelings in there, but it's hard to get to them, and / you're a challenge to try to find what you're feeling at any one moment./ You still will have a tendency, I think, to say something sharp./

7      T: If you were to express your feelings to that friend of your husband who was talking about "when I was working...," and implying that his wife did nothing equivalent taking care of the children and the household, what feeling would you have...how would you have labeled your feeling at that moment?/

P: I knew why his talk bothered me. He sounded so much like my husband Jim. I knew he hit a raw nerve.

7, 3      T: How did it make you feel? / And this is going to be a challenge for you./

P: Yeah. Right. How did it make me feel?

8, 4, 7      T: He reminded you of Jim, okay./ This is still intellectual./ How did he make you feel at that moment?/

P: The only thing I can think of is anger.

9, 6      T: You may have thought: "I feel angry at you for what you're saying."/ Now you don't say words like that? "I feel anger."/

P: No.

10, 5      T: I mean, you didn't even recognize it before./ But one of the ways that you might safely express the way you feel to someone is to say how you feel./

P: Oh, what a concept. (*laughs*)

8, 5, 4, 7      T: (*laughs*) Yes, what a concept./ So, I want to see if you could practice that a little bit. To put a label on it because you are slippery around your feelings./ At 48 you've learned a lot of ways to avoid how you feel. There's going to be some work in puncturing through your intellect to get to your emotions./ And, how do you feel about coughing in front of the TV camera?/

P: I don't like it. It'll be a terrible tape. (*cough*)

7     T: How does it make you feel?/

P: I don't know. I don't know if I have any feelings about that.

7     T: If someone else was doing something that would look bad, how do you think that person would feel?/

P: Maybe embarrassed, or ah . . . I basically feel like I'm way on past embarrassment, so (*coughs, coughs, coughs*) so I don't want to ruin the session by coughing all the way through it, so is that embarrassment? I don't know.

8, 4     T: Yeah, embarrassment,/ and maybe a little deeper than that./

P: When you come from as deeply dysfunctional a family as mine, boy you go farther than that to get embarrassed. (*cough*) You know . . .

13, 10, 7     T: No, I don't know. I don't know./ Maybe you don't have to go very far at all to get embarrassed too, which I think is more the case./ If someone was doing something that she couldn't control, that was gonna create embarrassment, how might she feel?/

P: (*cough*) Embarrassed, I guess. (*cough*)

6, 4, 6, 10, 4, 7     T: Frustrated? Helpless?/ These are down a little bit lower because you're not embarrassed yet. / Out of control? / These are words that get to feelings that you're not particularly familiar with. / To be able to struggle with feelings means you have to be able to recognize them./ When you were able to be loving to Jim, how did you feel?/

P: Of course, (*laughs*). I first felt loving when I was going to town and do the shopping and then to the family reunion. I bent down and kissed him and I probably, if anything, felt gratitude that he wasn't going to give me a lot of trouble about it. Because, usually when I leave the house, even though he normally doesn't verbally express anything, he acts as if I am doing something wrong or he'll say, "Yeah right." He is aware that I read his body language. I'm much better at other people's feelings than my own.

6     T: What are feelings that other people have?/

P: (*clears her throat*) Well, I know that Jim feels abandoned when I'm running out of the house and wonders why isn't he enough for me. Why do I have to see friends and family?

7     T: How does that make him feel, that you have to have other people?/

P: Well, it makes him feel sad and angry and . . . abandoned.

| | |
|---|---|
| 10, 4, 7 | T: Okay, sadness and anger are feelings that people have. You may even have such feelings./ Abandonment can lead to feelings of sadness and anger./ What other feelings do people have?/ <br> P: Oh, everything from joy, hysteria . . . |
| 8 | T: You do hysteria sometimes./ <br> P: Um hmm. (*yes*) |
| 4, 8, 14, 6 | T: Joy is a feeling, sadness, anger, hurt are other ones that people have./ So Jim felt hurt that you need to have other people in your life besides him./ All right./ How good are you at picking up your own sadness?/ <br> P: Oh, pretty good. |
| 6 | T: So, you know that one fairly well?/ <br> P: Um hmm. (*yes*) |
| 6 | T: How about telling people that you're sad./ <br> P: Oh, I don't have too much trouble with that. Ah, with the panic attacks, I have had to talk about my feelings, about feeling sad or hurt or ashamed. |
| 8, 9 | T: So, those feelings are more accessible to you and easier for you to talk about with people. / So anger is the one that you have the most difficulty with then./ <br> P: Um hmm. (*yes*) |
| 6 | T: How good are you at recognizing anger in other people?/ <br> P: Oh, yeah. Real good. |
| 8, 7 | T: You're sensitive to that one too, as I might imagine you would be./ What about being able to say to Jim, "I'm angry with you."/ <br> P: I can do that. |
| 6 | T: Have you done that before?/ <br> P: Oh, yeah. (*laughs*) No more than 10 million times, but it didn't do any good. |
| 7 | T: Now what's the difference between the way you are now about anger and the way you were before?/ <br> P: You mean when I was repressing it? |
| 10 | T: Yes. My impression was that you didn't express anger until it got intense./ <br> P: Um hmm. (*yes*) |
| 8, 6, 8, 10, 12, 8 | T: When you came back from Iowa and boom, blew up at him./ If you change, you may be able to say "I'm angry" over smaller things./ You sound like you may be able to say to him, "I care about you," too./ That other feeling may be coming to the surface as you get more comfortable with your own anger./ You're nodding,/ that's what you experienced recently with him./ <br> P: Um hmm. (*yes*) |

6

T: Do you care about Jim?/
P: Well, as the semantics go, I love Jim, I'm not sure I'm in love with Jim, but yes, I've always known I loved Jim, even when I was angry. But the "in love" romantic feeling is gone.

8, 6

T: But you do love him./ How often do you express that feeling to him?/
P: Well, it depends on how big a jerk he is (*laughs*). Since Jim is negative most of the time, I just talk about whatever's going on, which is what we may have for supper that night or what's going on with the kids or mother. So I just stick to daily subjects.

7

T: I'm curious about how this awareness of your anger is going to influence your relationship to him./
P: I feel the biggest reason I was on such a high as I wrote about anger, was because I was able to take a more clinical view and see everyone's patterns and see that I don't have to be controlled by mother or Jim, my grandmother, and my past. I do know it's going to take work, but at this point I don't give a damn what happens with Jim and I, whether we stay together or whether we break up. Because I finally realized that I am okay on my own, and I would rather be free and living in an efficiency apartment some-where than to live with Jim and feel miserable. So, basically I don't care.

14, 4, 7, 7

T: Okay./ One final question, and then we will stop for this time. Or two questions really./ What about the spring-summer business and not the winter? / What do you make out of that pattern?/
P: (*coughs*)

6, 7

T: You had your anxiety in the spring-summer but not during the winter?/ Hard to explain that one still?/
P: Yeah, after Pat (her chiropractor) did the emotional release thing on me, I started feeling better immediately. I felt better after I was here last time. I felt better as I began to feel like I had a right, if I want to be selfish today. If I want to say, "I'm not going to get out of my nightgown, I'm just gonna lie around, scratch where I want to," you know, then that's okay.

8, 4, 9

T: And that's where you are now. / And now there is an adventure in front of you./ You're not sure where this is going to take you, but you feel liberated and that feels good./
P: Um hmm. (*yes*)

7, 7

T: What about my role in this?/ What do you need from me in the future in regard to helping you?/
P: I don't know. I guess to keep me from going off the deep end. We still haven't really discussed the safer ways for me to express anger. I can always do the psychologist trick and turn it back around. I'm going to do that on mother the next time she

throws one of those fits or demands I do something. I'm going to say, "Mother, I do everything you ask me to, why do you have to be demanding?" Then I'll wait for a reaction. She'll probably throw another fit, but I'll keep asking her that question until maybe she'll say, "Well, that is true. I do get everything I want."

5, 4, 5, 3, 8, 3, 6    T: Well, you may be able to come up with these safer ways of doing them without much help from me./ So, as you know, I'm going to be on vacation for the next couple of weeks./ During that period of time I'd like you to write down examples of the safer expressions of anger. Let's see what you come up with. / You may come up with more than I ever could come up with because you've been so psychologically clever./ Now that you know that you need to develop safe ways of expressing something you are aware of,/ I think you will come up with a lot of good ones. So, I'd like to see what you come up with./ All right?

# ANSWERS TO FORM 6

## Hill's Sample Transcript

Each response unit is demarcated with a slash. Numbers immediately to the left of the transcript represent the averaged assessments of experienced professional therapists about the appropriate category for each response unit. Numbers in the far left column are keyed to the following categories: 1 = minimal encouragement, 2 = silence, 3 = approval-reassurance, 4 = information, 5 = direct guidance, 6 = closed question, 7 = open question, 8 = restatement, 9 = reflection, 10 = interpretation, 11 = confrontation, 12 = nonverbal referent, 13 = self-disclosure, 14 = other.

14, 7       CO: Hello./ Why don't you start out by telling me what is on your mind?/

              CL: I've just been feeling down lately./ I'm having a lot of trouble getting motivated and getting stuff done./ I haven't felt like going to class./ Nothing really interests me./

6       CO: What is your major?/

              CL: I haven't really decided on a major because I haven't found anything that turns me on./

6       CO: Are you living on campus?/

              CL: I'm living at home/ and I feel a lot of pressure on me./ I would like to live in the dorm/ but my parents won't pay for it/ and I don't have the money myself./

1       CO: MmHmm/

              CL: I mean, I live right near campus/ and they say why should you live in a dorm?/ You might as well live at home and save us money./ It is kind of a stifling feeling just being there./

8       CO: You would rather live in a dorm than at home right now./

              CL: I think I would feel more free in a dorm./ I just feel so restricted at home, like they're watching my every move/ and I don't feel free to come and go as I please./ For example, if you want to go out, they always tell me to stay out as late as I want and do what I want, but then the next day they're always asking and checking up on me./ I shouldn't have to put up with that any more at my age./

9       CO: You're angry because they treat you like a little kid./

              CL: Yeah./ I'm not sure how to deal with that./ They're providing me with a place to sleep and helping me out a little with school/ so I feel like I can't say anything to them./

8       CO: It sounds like you think that you have to stay home and do what they want./

              CL: Yeah,/ but it's killing my social life./ It's not really what I want to do./ It's even having a bad effect on my schoolwork./

Reprinted with permission from Hill, C. E. (1986). An overview of the Hill Counselor and Client Verbal Response Modes Category Systems. In Greenberg, L. S., & Pinsof, W. M. (Eds.), *The Psychotherapeutic Process* (pp. 131–159). New York: Guilford Press.

| | | |
|---|---|---|
| 9 | CO: | I hear you saying that you would feel freer to live your own life if you weren't living at home./ |
| | CL: | That's true./ But the problem with that is money./ I'm going to school part-time and working part-time and don't have enough money for a dorm or an apartment./ My parents won't give me any more money either./ What really burns me up is that my younger brother is not in school and works and they don't give him any of this crap./ |
| 1 | CO: | I see./ |
| | CL: | (*pause = 8 seconds*)/ He can do anything he wants, you know, in terms of living at home./ They don't bug him at all about what he's doing and where he's going./ I guess they think that because I'm the oldest and more responsible, I can handle more than he can./ They both had a hard time as kids and they really want me to have what they didn't have./ I guess they think I've got a better chance than my brother does to succeed/ and so they're tougher on me./ |
| 12, 9 | CO: | Your voice is very loud right now./ You must be very resentful./ |
| | CL: | Well, I just don't want to live their lives for them./ I want to have some fun on my own./ |
| 2, 8, 11 | CO: | (*silence = 5 seconds*)/ You say you want to move out/ yet you don't./ |
| | CL: | I guess I don't want to disappoint them./ Um, they'd feel real bad if I left/ and |
| 10 | CO: | (*pause = 3 seconds* / I wonder if you're afraid of making the big step of growing up by moving out?/ |
| | CL: | I hadn't thought of it that way./ I don't know if that's exactly it./ I think I'm pretty independent./ |
| 4, 8, 11 | CO: | Well, let's look at that for a minute./ You say you're independent/ but when your parents tell you to do all these things, you do them./ |
| | CL: | What else can I do?/ What choice do you think I have?/ I'm living there/ and the rule is that I should do what they say as long as I live under their roof./ They might kick me out if I didn't./ |
| 13, 13, 13, 10 | CO: | You know, when I was your age I had a very difficult time leaving home./ My father had died and my mother was all alone./ I felt guilty for a long time about leaving her./ I wonder if you're feeling some guilt about growing up and leaving them!/ |
| | CL: | Well, I do feel guilty about leaving but also angry at them for making me feel this way and for treating my brother differently./ What do you think I ought to do to resolve this?/ |
| 5 | CO: | Maybe it would be a good idea to drop out of school for awhile, get a job, and make enough money to move into your own apartment./ |

|   |   |
|---|---|
| | CL: I've thought about that but feel anxious that I'd never go back to school./ But you know, as I think about it, maybe the reason I have so much trouble about motivation in school is because of these conflicts with my parents./ |
| 7 | CO: What do you mean?/ |
| | CL: Well, if I feel like I'm doing everything for them instead of because I want to do it and if there's always this battle over my future, it's pretty hard for me to figure out what I want./ |
| 12 | CO: When you said that, your forehead wrinkled up and you began to look tearful./ |
| | CL: (*silence = 10 seconds*)/ |
| 4, 7 | CO: We only have a couple of minutes left./ Where would you like to go from here with this problem?/ |
| | CL: Do you think it would be worthwhile to talk to someone again?/ |
| 7 | CO: What do you think?/ |
| | CL: You've made me think about some things./ I'm feeling really confused right now./ I wasn't sure before this about seeing you because I didn't know what to expect from this counseling/ but you seem to understand me./ Maybe you can help me figure out some of this mess with my parents and school./ |
| 1, 10, 3, 3 | CO: Yeah./ It sounds like you have trouble figuring out who you are and what you want out of your life, separate from what your parents want./ That certainly seems like something appropriate to talk about here in counseling./ I think it would be a good idea for you to continue to see me./ |
| | CL: I do feel a bit anxious talking to you because it feels like you can see right through me./ |
| 13, 13, 3, 3 | CO: I feel somewhat anxious right now too./ I usually feel a little tense until I get to know a person and decide whether we can work together./ I think you did the right thing by coming in at this point in your life./ You'll probably feel better after talking about your concerns./ |
| | CL: I hope so./ I think I'll go home and think about some of these things./ Maybe I'll think about my options about moving out and where I could afford to live./ Maybe I'll talk some to my parents about moving out./ Does that sound like a good idea to you?/ |
| 5, 4, 4 | CO: Why don't we talk through that at your next session./ We need to stop now./ I'll see you next week at the same time./ |
| | CL: Great./ Thank you so much./ Have a nice day./ |
| 14, 14, 14 | CO: You too./ It's really beautiful weather out./ Feels like spring./ |
| | CL: It sure does./ Bye now./ |

## ANSWERS TO FORM 8

### Transcripts of Dr. Beitman's Session
### (Rating Intentions)

The numbers refer to the following categories: 1 = Set limits, 2 = Get information, 3 = Give information, 4 = Support, 5 = Focus, 6 = Clarify, 7 = Hope, 8 = Cathart, 9 = Cognitions, 10 = Behaviors, 11 = Self-control, 12 = Feelings, 13 = Insight, 14 = Change, 15 = Reinforce change, 16 = Resistance, 17 = Challenge, 18 = Relationship, 19 = Therapist needs, 20 = interpersonal.

*To the group leader*: We separated each intention by an asterisk (*), which does not occur in trainee's Form 12. This may facilitate your discussion with the group.

| | |
|---|---|
| 2 | T: I gave you a homework assignment last time. How many pages do we have here?*<br>P: Oh, probably 50. |
| 6 | T: Probably 50. And the homework assignment was to? What was the homework assignment?*<br>P: Oh, about anger. |
| 6 | T: What about anger?*<br>P: Describe my feelings about anger. |
| 2 | T: Your feelings about anger. And, what happened?*<br>P: As I began writing, I just went ohoooooo, and all these things from my childhood popped out, and I got in touch with my anger. (*laughs*) |
| 12 | T: (*laughs*) You got in touch with your anger.*<br>P: Yea, I got in touch with my anger. |
| 15, 12 | T: It was my impression last time that you were skating on top of it but never or rarely visiting it.* So this week you got in touch with your anger. What was that like for you?*<br>P: Well, at first when I was keeping the anger log, I was surprised, but then as I watched my pattern I noticed anger would arise and immediately I would squash it. (*coughs*) And so, I think it was Thursday when my mother was doing a number on me at the hospital, and I just said that's enough. And so, (*coughs*) |
| 4 | T: Do you want some water?*<br>P: Yeah, maybe it would be good. I'm sorry. And ah, then I called both my sisters and I said that I was going to take a day or two off from going to the hospital. (*cough, cough*) Mother, she is ill, she is dying, but I never failed to do anything she asked me to do, but she begins demanding (*pounds fist on chair*), throwing fits like a three year old, you know, and "You, give me that," and I thought she wanted her tissues so I handed her the tissues. "No, no," but she wanted the lid that went on the hotplate. And so, when I gave her the tissues she threw it and "no, no, no" she says, and she is still pointing. |

4      T: All right.*

P: So I stood up to her. I put the tissues back on the tray and I said, "Well, damn Mother, don't wait a minute, that would be awful." And she looked at me like "what's going on here?".

15, 12      T: So you told your mother to cool it. And that's a new experience for you. A relatively new experience for you. * So you at that moment decided not to go after what she was asking you to do. Now, I'm curious about what that felt like for you too.*

P: Well, at the time I was just angry. I wasn't into evaluating myself. I was just angry.

6      T: Just angry.*

P: At that moment, I decided I was doing part of this homework assignment, that I had a right to anger as much as anyone else. If other people are angry, I make excuses for them. They're tired, sick, or something. And then I realized, well how many of them make excuses for you? How many are willing to say, "Oh, you're angry."

6      T: If you express some kind of irritation.*

P: Um hmm. (*yes*)

6      T: You wrote in your diary that when you were growing up you were not permitted to have anger.*

P: The messages to me in my childhood were that I had no right to my feelings. One time, I was lying on the bed crying, and my mother said, "What's the matter with you?" And I said, "I'm just so lonely." And she said, "Oh, hell you can't be lonely, you're with kids at school all day."

6      T: So she rejected your feelings.*

P: Right.

6      T: She said your feelings don't count. *

P: I grew up feeling ugly, dumb, lazy, because I couldn't be tired because children don't get tired. I was just lazy. I always figured my father was my buddy because he would sit down and talk to me. But what my father did was philosophize. If I was angry I should understand this person and well, you know, he had a bad marriage, or he was hurt in an accident . . .

13      T: So, your father gave you a model for how to make excuses for other people's feelings and bad behavior, and then you started being able to apply that way of thinking to yourself.*

P: Um hmm. (*yes*)

6      T: You've had more feelings in yourself this week than you have for quite a while. Well, what's that been like for you?*

P: Well, after I stayed up all Friday night writing this, I began to see these patterns and realized that a child comes into the world as a clean slate and then people start writing on it. And so many of these beliefs that had been pounded into my head were not my beliefs. I felt like there was a chance for me to be free of them to think my own thoughts. It felt great!

6   T: You seem to describe feeling liberated from other people's imposed rules and attitudes on you, and that was a very wonderful feeling for you.*

     P: Um hmm. (*yes*)

         * * *

15, 14, 6  T: And, now you're entering a phase where you're going to be able to express anger differently from before.* Maybe you will need to be able to say something like, "I'm angry," to somebody. Or, "What you said has made me feel angry." * I keep trying to find ways to label your feelings, but I have difficulty.*

     P: (*coughs*) I'm slippery. (*laughs*)

14, 12, 10  T: You're slippery.* Yeah, there are feelings in there, but it's hard to get to them, and you're a challenge to try to find what you're feeling at any one moment.* You still will have a tendency, I think, to say something sharp.*

12   T: If you were to express your feelings to that friend of your husband who was talking about "when I was working...," and implying that his wife did nothing equivalent taking care of the children and the household, what feeling would you have... how would you have labeled your feeling at that moment? *

     P: I knew why his talk bothered me. He sounded so much like my husband Jim. I knew he hit a raw nerve.

12, 14  T: How did it make you feel? * And this is going to be a challenge for you.*

     P: Yeah. Right. How did it make me feel?

12   T: He reminded you of Jim, okay. This is still intellectual. How did he make you feel at that moment?*

     P: The only thing I can think of is anger.

14   T: You may have thought: "I feel angry at you for what you're saying." Now you don't say words like that? "I feel anger." *

     P: No.

15, 14  T: I mean, you didn't even recognize it before. * But one of the ways that you might safely express the way you feel to someone is to say how you feel.*

     P: Oh, what a concept. (*laughs*)

14, 12  T: (*laughs*) Yes, what a concept. So, I want to see if you could practice that a little bit. To put a label on it because you are slippery around your feelings. At 48 you've learned a lot of ways to avoid how you feel. There's going to be some work in puncturing through your intellect to get to your emotions.* And, how do you feel about coughing in front of the TV camera? *

     P: I don't like it. It'll be a terrible tape. (*cough*)

12   T: How does it make you feel? *

     P: I don't know. I don't know if I have any feelings about that.

12   T: If someone else was doing something that would look bad, how do you think that person would feel? *

P: Maybe embarrassed, or ah ... I basically feel like I'm way on past embarrassment, so (*coughs, coughs, coughs*) so I don't want to ruin the session by coughing all the way through it, so is that embarrassment? I don't know.

12   T: Yeah, embarrassment, and maybe a little deeper than that. *

P: When you come from as deeply dysfunctional a family as mine, boy you go farther than that to get embarrassed. (*cough*) You know ...

12   T: No, I don't know. I don't know. Maybe you don't have to go very far at all to get embarrassed too, which I think is more the case. If someone was doing something that she couldn't control, that was gonna create embarrassment, how might she feel? *

P: (*cough*) Embarrassed, I guess. (*cough*)

12, 13, 12   T: Frustrated? Helpless? These are down a little bit lower because you're not embarrassed yet. Out of control? These are words that get to feelings that you're not particularly familiar with.* To be able to struggle with feelings means you have to be able to recognize them.* When you were able to be loving to Jim, how did you feel? *

P: Of course, (*laughs*) I first felt loving when I was going to town and do the shopping and then to the family reunion. I bent down and kissed him and I probably, if anything, felt gratitude that he wasn't going to give me a lot of trouble about it. Because, usually when I leave the house, even though he normally doesn't verbally express anything, he acts as if I am doing something wrong or he'll say, "Yeah right." He is aware that I read his body language. I'm much better at other people's feelings than my own.

2   T: What are feelings that other people have? *

P: (*clears her throat*) Well, I know that Jim feels abandoned when I'm running out of the house and wonders why isn't he enough for me. Why do I have to see friends and family?

2   T: How does that make him feel, that you have to have other people? *

P: Well, it makes him feel sad and angry and ... abandoned.

12   T: Okay, sadness and anger are feelings that people have. You may even have such feelings. Abandonment can lead to feelings of sadness and anger. What other feelings do people have? *

P: Oh, everything from joy, hysteria ...

10   T: You do hysteria sometimes. *

P: Um hmm. (*yes*)

12   T: Joy is a feeling, sadness, anger, hurt are other ones that people have. So Jim felt hurt that you need to have other people in your life besides him. All right. How good are you at picking up your own sadness? *

P: Oh, pretty good.

12   T: So, you know that one fairly well?*

P: Um hmm. (*yes*)

10   T: How about telling people that you're sad.*

P: Oh, I don't have too much trouble with that. Ah, with the panic attacks, I have had to talk about my feelings, about feeling sad or hurt or ashamed.

6   T: So, those feelings are more accessible to you and easier for you to talk about with people. So anger is the one that you have the most difficulty with then.*

P: Um hmm. (*yes*)

12   T: How good are you at recognizing anger in other people? *

P: Oh, yeah. Real good.

4, 10   T: You're sensitive to that one too, as I might imagine you would be.* What about being able to say to Jim, "I'm angry with you."*

P: I can do that.

2   T: Have you done that before?*

P: Oh, yeah. (*laughs*) No more than 10 million times, but it didn't do any good.

13   T: Now what's the difference between the way you are now about anger and the way you were before?*

P: You mean when I was repressing it?

13   T: Yes. My impression was that you didn't express anger until it got intense.*

P: Um hmm. (*yes*)

14, 15   T: When you came back from Iowa and boom, blew up at him. If you change, you may be able to say "I'm angry" over smaller things.* You sound like you may be able to say to him, "I care about you," too. That other feeling may be coming to the surface as you get more comfortable with your own anger. You're nodding, that's what you experienced recently with him.*

P: Um hmm. (*yes*)

2   T: Do you care about Jim?*

P: Well, as the semantics go I love Jim, I'm not sure I'm in love with Jim, but yes, I've always known I loved Jim, even when I was angry. But the "in love" romantic feeling is gone.

6, 10   T: But you do love him.* How often do you express that feeling to him?*

P: Well, it depends on how big a jerk he is? (*laughs*) Since Jim is negative most of the time, I just talk about whatever's going on, which is what we may have for supper that night or what's going on with the kids or mother. So I just stick to daily subjects.

14   T: I'm curious about how this awarencess of your anger is going to influence your relationship to him. *

P: I feel the biggest reason I was on such a high as I wrote about anger, was because I was able to take a more clinical view and see everyone's patterns and see that I don't have to be controlled by mother or Jim, my grandmother, and my past. I do know it's going to take work, but at this point I don't give a damn what happens with Jim and I, whether we stay together or whether we break up. Because I finally realized that I am okay on my own, and I would rather be free and living in an efficiency apartment somewhere than to live with Jim and feel miserable. So, basically I don't care.

2      T: Okay. One final question, and then we will stop for this time. Or two questions really. What about the spring-summer business and not the winter? What do you make out of that pattern?*

       P: (*coughs*)

6      T: You had your anxiety in the spring-summer but not during the winter? Hard to explain that one still.*

       P: Yeah, after Pat [her chiropractor] did the emotional release thing on me, I started feeling better immediately. I felt better after I was here last time. I felt better as I began to feel like I had a right, if I want to be selfish today. If I want to say, "I'm not going to get out of my nightgown, I'm just gonna lie around, scratch where I want to," you know, then that's okay.

4, 15  T: And that's where you are now. And now there is an adventure in front of you.* You're not sure where this is going to take you, but you feel liberated and that feels good.*

       P: Um hmm. (*yes*)

18, 19 T: What about my role in this?* What do you need from me in the future in regard to helping you?*

       P: I don't know. I guess to keep me from going off the deep end. We still haven't really discussed the safer ways for me to express anger. I can always do the psychologist trick and turn it back around. I'm going to do that on mother the next time she throws one of those fits or demands I do something. I'm going to say, "Mother, I do everthing you ask me to, why do you have to be demanding?" Then I'll wait for a reaction. She'll probably throw another fit, but I'll keep asking her that question until maybe she'll say, "Well, that is true. I do get everything I want."

15, 3, 15 T: Well, you may be able to come up with these safer ways of doing them without much help from me.* So, as you know, I'm going to be on vacation for the next couple of weeks.* During that period of time I'd like you to write down examples of the safer expressions of anger. Let's see what you come up with. You may come up with more than I ever could come up with because you've been so psychologically clever. Now that you know that you need to develop safe ways of expressing something you are aware of, I think you will come up with a lot of good ones. So, I'd like to see what you come up with. All right?

# MODULE **3**

# *Working Alliance*

## SESSIONS

### Session 1

Purpose: To review the text of Module 3 in *Learning Psychotherapy, Second Edition*. The working alliance introduces trainees to the process of engagement in the psychotherapy relationship and demonstrates the value of psychotherapy research.

**1.** Focusing on Bordin's concept of working alliance (Bordin, 1979), group discussion can help trainees develop a theoretical understanding of the working alliance in psychotherapy. After this discussion, distribute Form 9 (Working Alliance Inventory, WAI) to each trainee. Ask trainees to guess the category of each item: *task, bond,* or *goal*.

Play the tape of Dr. Rogers's session (Shostrom, 1965) for about 10 minutes and then choose two items from each of the three subscales of the WAI to discuss. Ask trainees to rate each item based on what appears on the tape, and to justify the rating. If the trainees misunderstand the items, provide clarification. They are being trained to behave like research associates and to think like researchers about their own efforts. This step can help trainees improve inter-rater reliability. In the real world of research training, these sessions would take much longer and go into much greater depth to obtain inter-rater reliability. Research training promotes "stepping back" from experience in order to objectify observations, in this way promoting activation of the observing self.

You should minimize the inevitable discussion about Rogers's theoretical orientation and therapeutic style because of time constraints. Guide the discussion to focus on your trainees' understanding of working alliance, rather than on the patient's problem. The discussion should focus on the differences between the Bordin concept of working alliance and other relationship components (such as Rogers's emphasis on the therapist's empathy, Strong's emphasis on the patient's belief in the therapist's ability, and any other perspectives you have).

**2.** Trainees often have trouble discriminating between *tasks* and *goals*. Clarification of these two terms can lead to better understanding of working alliance. Discuss methods for establishing and strengthening *bonds*.

**3.** Homework: Arrange for trainees to view the Rogers's tape and ask them to use Form 9 (WAI) to rate the working alliance individually without discussion with colleagues. Make a copy for each trainee.

## Session 2

Purpose: To review trainees' WAI ratings of Rogers's tape and discuss Rogers's style. While rating the therapist's words and behavior, trainees examine in fine detail the concept of working alliance.

**1.** During the first 40 minutes, the group members discuss their feelings and thoughts about Dr. Rogers's session. The discussion is facilitated by asking trainees to report and then explain their ratings of specific items. Differences among them serve as discussion triggers. Topics to target include: Dr. Rogers's working alliance, with emphasis on how he establishes and maintains the therapeutic bond, his style of therapy, and perhaps his reactions to Gloria in the session, including his suggestion that he might like to be a father to her.

During the second 20 minutes, show part of the videotape of Dr. Beitman's third session with MF to the trainees, again using Form 9, WAI. After playing about 10 minutes of the tape of Dr. Beitman's session for the group, choose two items from each of the three subscales of the WAI to discuss. Based on what they just saw, trainees are asked to rate each item and justify their rating. This helps you determine if any trainees are misunderstanding individual items, which can then be clarified.

**2.** Our trainees easily agree that bonds are strong between Rogers and Gloria, but there are sometimes arguments about whether tasks are defined and agreed upon. Some say definitely "yes," because at the end Rogers makes it clear that it is up to Gloria to decide, and some say "no," because the steps she needs to take in order to change have not been defined. There is somewhat more consensus that goals are agreed upon, but when trainees are asked what the goals are, they cannot easily define them.

Trainees often wonder about Rogers's level of activity and speculate that this is probably an early form of psychotherapy. They are not bothered by Rogers's implication that he might like to be her father. Nor are they bothered by the fact that Rogers and Gloria maintained a relationship by writing letters to one another. They are interested in knowing about a lawsuit by Gloria's daughter for misuse of the film, which has been shown in many, many training programs.

Some trainees are impressed with his effective use of silence.

**3.** Homework: Trainees are asked to watch Beitman's whole session and then rate the working alliance.

## Session 3

Purpose: To review WAI responses to the Beitman tape.

**1.** The seminar leader asks trainees to describe their thoughts and feelings about Beitman's session. The discussion can be facilitated by asking each trainee to select a specific item, and then asking all trainees to explain their ratings and discuss differences. In addition, they can be asked to indicate which subscale the item belongs to. The discussion should include the nature of Beitman's working alliance, with special reference to the three subscales, and the differences between Rogers and Beitman.

**2.** Our trainees are generally interested in the different level of activity between Rogers and Beitman. They ask about the evolution of psychotherapy and note that patients expect more active interventions now compared to the early 1960s. Agreement on tasks for Beitman's session is easier to reach than for Rogers's session.

**3.** There is no trainee homework, but there is homework for the group leader. After this session, compile the statistics of trainees' ratings for Rogers's and Beitman's working alliances, as well as the WAI from the trainees' and their patients' ratings of working alliance of the third sessions during pretraining. Here are the subscales of WAI and the polarity of items that you will use in your statistics. For a positive polarity (+), simply add the score; for a negative polarity (−), subtract the score from 8 and then add the result.

### Scoring Key for the WAI

#### 36 Items:

| | |
|---|---|
| Task scale: | 2, 4, 7, 11, 13, 15, 16, 18, 24, 31, 33, 35. |
| Polarity | + + − − + − + + + − − + |
| Bond scale: | 1, 5, 8, 17, 19, 20, 21, 23, 26, 28, 29, 36. |
| Polarity | − + + + + − + + + + − + |
| Goal scale: | 3, 6, 9, 10, 12, 14, 22, 25, 27, 30, 32, 34. |
| Polarity | − + − − − + + + − + + − |

#### 12 Items: (the polarity of all items except 9 and 11 is "+") (Found in Pretraining)

| | |
|---|---|
| Task scale: | 1, 2, 3, 4. |
| Bond scale: | 5, 6, 7, 8. |
| Goal Scale: | −9, 10, −11, 12. |

## Session 4

Purpose: To review statistics on working alliance (Rogers, Beitman).

**1.** Following are tables describing the results of WAI ratings from several different groups from the University of Missouri. Show to your trainees the group scores of the WAI rating of the two therapists. This is intended to be a more objective rating of each therapist. You can use the data provided in Tables 3–1, 3–2, 3–3, and 3–4 to demonstrate differences between your current trainees and other groups. The groups that rated Rogers include three groups of residents (at University of Missouri) being trained in this program, and one group composed of psychiatric faculty members. Of note in the Rogers ratings is the consistency of total score across three of the four groups (Group 1 was somewhat higher than the rest; we explain this in part by the fact that Group 1 rated the working alliance as Module 2 rather than Module 3). Also, all groups rated Rogers highest on the "bonds" subscale. Two groups of residents and the faculty group rated Dr. Beitman's working alliance. In addition, Dr. Beitman and his patient rated the working alliance; their total scores were almost identical. Each trainee can compare his or her own ratings of Rogers and Beitman with those of other trainees, as well as to the group averages.

### UMC Residents' and Faculty's Rating of Working Alliance

**2.** How do the trainees explain the differences between the other group ratings and their own? Perhaps differences are related to how closely Rogers and Beitman matched the trainee's own style or how the rater felt about the interaction. Beitman's differences from Rogers might be explained by (1) Beitman's being closer to recent conventions in the practice of psychotherapy, i.e., he is more active; (2) Beitman's having had three

**TABLE 3–1   Working Alliance of Dr. Rogers's Session (36 Items)**

|  | Group One | Group Two | Group Three | Faculty |
|---|---|---|---|---|
| X | 218.63 | 192.50 | 197.86 | 187.17 |
| SD | 14.13 | 20.40 | 19.95 | 20.73 |
| N | 8 | 4 | 7 | 6 |

**TABLE 3–2   Subscales of Dr. Rogers's Working Alliance**

|  | Group One | Group Two | Group Three | Faculty |
|---|---|---|---|---|
| Task X | 71.63 | 59.50 | 66.14 | 57.50 |
| SD | 4.96 | 8.67 | 8.80 | 7.87 |
| Bond X | 78.00 | 72.75 | 69.86 | 71.33 |
| SD | 4.2 | 3.78 | 7.29 | 3.01 |
| Goals X | 69.00 | 57.25 | 61.86 | 56.67 |
| SD | 7.71 | 11.30 | 8.03 | 12.61 |

**TABLE 3–3   Working Alliance of Dr. Beitman's Session (36 Items)**

|  | Group two | Group three | Faculty | Beitman | Patient |
|---|---|---|---|---|---|
| X | 210.00 | 223.86 | 198.00 | 234 | 232 |
| SD | 7.44 | 11.20 | 20.4 |  |  |
| N | 4 | 7 | 11 |  |  |

**TABLE 3–4   Subscales of Dr. Beitman's Working Alliance**

|  | Group two | Group three | Faculty | Beitman | Patient |
|---|---|---|---|---|---|
| Task X | 69.75 | 74.43 | 66.60 | 76 | 80 |
| SD | 3.00 | 3.82 | 7.10 |  |  |
| Bond X | 71.75 | 76.86 | 66.70 | 81 | 70 |
| SD | 6.40 | 5.58 | 7.70 |  |  |
| Goals X | 68.50 | 72.57 | 64.60 | 77 | 82 |
| SD | 3.31 | 4.54 | 6.90 |  |  |

sessions with his patient at the time of taping, while Rogers was meeting Gloria for first time; (3) trainees' possible preference for Beitman because they knew him; (4) possibly the order in which tapes were rated.

During the session, you have also presented the results of trainees' ratings of the working alliance from their pretraining session. Differences between the patient's and therapist's rating of the same working alliance can indicate excessive modesty or confidence. If one trainee-patient pair shares a notable discrepancy, the group might begin the exercise by guessing who the trainee is. Comparing the patient's rating with the therapist's can help trainees to become aware of how patients and therapists sometimes perceive the working alliance differently. Since this perception varies from one patient to another, trainees will have to know which scores belong to which of their two patients. When comparing the trainee rating with Rogers/Beitman ratings, keep in mind that the trainees are using a 12-item scale, while Rogers/Beitman was a 36-item scale. For example, the Rogers rating of 210 translates into a 12-item rating of 70. Outside observers, therapists, and patients almost inevitably rate the same event differently.

From this discussion, trainees gain the following:

1. They learn that as beginners they should be emphasizing bond formation.
2. They begin to see what abilities they will have to develop later in defining tasks and building therapeutic bonds.
3. They begin to identify themselves as *bond* people, *task* people, or *goal* people.
4. The numerical ratings help them to feel that they have actually done something with their patients.

Without proposing answers, we raise the question of whether a resident's own predisposition to establishing bonds, tasks, or goals influenced the way they rated. We also ask about their current predispositions and what strengths they would like to develop.

**3.** Homework: Ask trainees to review the Exploitation Index (Form 10–1), the Description of Exploitation Index (Form 10–2), and Boundary Violation Role Play (Form 10–3).

## Session 5

Purpose: To have trainees complete GI (Post-Module 3a) and COSE (Post-Module 3b) in the first 20 minutes. In the remaining 40 minutes, review the subscales of the Exploitation Index, which consists of seven subscales that explore the therapist's behaviors, thoughts, and feelings beyond the professional role. This discussion is intended to help trainees increase their awareness of boundary issues and give them the opportunity to examine their own behaviors toward any particular patient. Complete the Global Impressions of Trainees Change (GITC) after this session.

1. After the trainees complete COSE and GI, the group discusses the subcategories and the items on the Form 10–1 and Form 10–2. The definition of each subscale is read aloud and discussed. Each trainee should offer comments. Discussion should include delineating those items that seem too rigid and those items that point to necessary boundaries. This discussion should help the trainees be aware of and understand boundary violations. The group then performs Boundary Violation Role Play.
2. The discussions in our training include:

a. General boundary violations. Many disagree with the prohibitions on accepting referrals from patients or friends. We recognize that these are relatively rigid requirements, for which there may be occasional well-justified exceptions.
b. Eroticism. Discussion of the mechanism by which "the therapist consciously and unconsciously molds the patient into an ideal sexual partner" requires subtlety beyond most trainees' experience, and usually leads to further discussion of countertransference. This topic is reserved for Module 7.
c. Exhibitionism. This serves as an example of using the patient to satisfy one's own needs and conflicts. What can a therapist talk about appropriately with a patient?

d. Dependency. Silence and tardiness are confusing examples for the trainees, but residents understand that some therapists will strive for heroic endurance of patient resistance to keep the patient feeling fully and completely accepted.

e. Power. When to direct (medications, homework, involuntary hospitalization), and when to collaborate. Some trainees recognize their desire to control and be in authority.

f. Greed. Many managed care plans require that a primary provider refer only to a specialist within the provider group. This often deprives patients of access to more capable therapists working in other groups. This illustrates the ethical dilemma of managed care, as residents may be torn between patient care and financial gain.

g. Enabling. Trainees see the enabling therapist as one who endures all the negative responses a patient can present without setting boundaries or considering termination. It is similar to dependency.

h. Boundary Violation Role Play. Residents at first were reluctant to consider confronting their patients, whether in medication management, or combined medications with psychotherapy or psychotherapy alone. They were happy the patient did not show. After some discussion they became convinced that there were good reasons for the confrontation. They then discovered that patients lie (e.g., I had a doctor's appointment and forgot about calling you), they have funny, demeaning reasons (e.g., my cat was sick so I took her to the vet), they become offended (e.g., I'm so busy and everyone keeps making demands on me) or they willingly step back to look at what is going on and appreciate the information.

**3.** Homework: Ask trainees to preview Module 4 text in *Learning Psychotherapy, Second Edition.*

# MODULE 4

# *Inductive Reasoning to Determine Patterns*

## SESSIONS

### Session 1

Purpose: To review the text of Module 4 in *Learning Psychotherapy, Second Edition*. You should spend the last 15 minutes discussing the "cherry pie" case in the introduction of Form 11–1.

**1.** The discussion should focus on the use of inductive reasoning to define maladaptive (as well as adaptive) patterns. You can offer one or two examples of the thought processes involved in pattern induction. In this module, we present three levels of patterns. First-level patterns are used most frequently by trainees to label patients' problems. We don't emphasize first-level patterns, however, first because trainees are often familiar with them, and second because the patterns do not clearly delineate what patients need to change. Level-two patterns are based in the theoretic modalities of psychotherapy; they are described in Appendix I. Study of these patterns helps trainees to develop their own theories of mind as they begin the lifelong exercise of sharpening their ideas about the ways human beings think and feel. However clear these models of mind are to trainees, they are useless unless they can be applied to actual patients in the context of treatment. Level three defines patterns that suggest to both therapist and patient what must be done to change the pattern.

**2.** In this training program, the discussion often begins with "What is a dysfunctional pattern?" and continues with a collaboration between patient and therapist about the meaning of *dysfunctional*, recognizing that each person may have a different sense of the concept and its applications.

**3.** Homework: The group members review Form 11–1 (Inductive Reasoning to Determine Patterns) as they begin to learn how to develop their ability to identify patterns (e.g., diagnoses), allowing about 15 minutes. We encourage them to think like physicians. For example, if, during a physical examination, the physician detects pain over the right upper quadrant of the abdomen, he/she will pursue diagnostic possibilities related to the liver. In the same way, painful, odd, or unusual thoughts, feelings, and/or behaviors serve as clues to psychological patterns. In this exercise, the trainees attempt to induce general patterns from the case vignettes without discussing them with colleagues or friends.

## Session 2

Purpose: To discuss Form 11–1. This session is intended to guide trainees' thinking in defining patients' patterns and to encourage them to formulate the pattern demonstrated in the vignette in terms that the patient can understand. You might also take this opportunity to demonstrate general principles of mental functioning in the vignettes. Trainees do not need to know the school patterns to do level III.

**1.** The group discusses the 10 vignettes (Form 11–1) from which the trainees have already derived the patterns as homework. If some trainees have not completed the homework assignment, the group may briefly discuss the possible reasons as an illustration of the reasons patients do not do homework. The trainees discuss the patterns they induced and explain their results within the group. There may be disagreements, which you will encourage the group to discuss. The discussion should be directed to the different levels of patterns. You can use the answers to Form 11–1 to facilitate the discussion.

**2.** Trainees usually grasp the idea of pattern induction fairly easily, but they tend to use first-level patterns, such as *low self-esteem* and *paranoid*, to describe patients. They struggle with describing the pattern to the patient. Stress the importance of studying the patterns and describing them in words that a patient could understand.

Figure 4–1 contains an incomplete list of inducing points. Trainees added: religious events, "hot cognitions," reactions to current events, dreams and intrusions.

During this discussion, trainees begin to see that patients have developed maladaptive patterns for specific, future-directed reasons, which might be called the patient intentions behind the patterns (e.g., fear of rejection, fear of conflict, fear of being blamed, fear of self-expression). Defining the feared, anticipated, desired consequence becomes part of the pattern definition. We attempt to keep the discussion at the surface, staying within the limited data of each vignette. After defining the pattern, we then encourage trainees to look for unconscious conflicts, hidden motives, automatic thoughts, interpersonal patterns, and triggers of old painful memories. Many simply try to order the patient to change rather than describing the pattern and implying what should be done.

**3.** Homework: Ask trainees to complete Form 12–1 (Transcripts for Inductive Reasoning). You may bring in speakers to elaborate on specific schools.

## Session 3

Purpose: To review Form 12–1. In this exercise, trainees formulate patients' patterns from dialogues. Transcripts have more information, more closely resemble the real world, and therefore present greater challenges in detecting patterns.

**1.** You may want to test a variety of perspectives from different theoretical schools of therapy to explore these patients. Ask trainees to not only describe the pattern, but to pretend to convey it to the patient as well. Each trainee should have an opportunity to report and discuss possible patterns induced from the transcripts.

**2.** In our training program, we intentionally keep this discussion loose and free-flowing in order to give trainees a chance to think flexibly together (a kind of antidote to *DSM-IV* categorical thinking).

**3.** Homework: The group goes to Form 13 (Triple-column Diary). It takes five or ten minutes to introduce the triple-column techniques (Beck, Rush, Shaw, & Emery, 1979). The group discusses how to assign the homework to patients. Emphasize that the therapist should help patients understand that it is their responsibility, and in their best interests, to do the homework. You should mention how to deal with possible patient reactions. For example, patients might refuse to do the homework. What are some possible reasons?

Therapists must avoid criticizing patients and instead explore with them reasons for not doing the homework. This may constitute another inducing point.

We recommend that for a one week period trainees use the triple-column diary to record their own feelings (e.g., excessive anger), unwanted thoughts (e.g., excessive self-criticism), or maladaptive behavior (e.g., smoking) associated with specific events.

## Session 4

Purpose: To review Form 13. We ask trainees to use the triple-column diary themselves, rather than with their patients, for the following reasons: (1) The triple-column technique is a structured homework exercise that promotes ongoing self-observation in patients who agree to do it. This exercise provides one of several ways to teach patients how to self-observe. By completing the exercise, trainees learn the details of the technique, and will then be better able to teach their patients how to use it to best advantage. (2) One of the goals of this training program is to stimulate the "observing self" within each trainee. The triple-column exercise helps trainees develop their ability to observe how they think and feel about themselves as therapists as they process patient information. By studying their own inductive reasoning processes, trainees refine their ability to monitor and direct their thinking.

**1.** Trainees discuss their triple-column diaries within the group and attempt to articulate their personal patterns.

**2.** Trainees report that, by doing this homework, they become aware of automatic thoughts. One trainee defined a pattern of excessive self-doubt (he was twice late to meetings and was rejected by a patient for being a trainee) and recorded his automatic thoughts of self-criticism and fear of being punished by others. Another described angry arguments with his wife about money, and realized through the diary how each of them was bringing unique attitudes toward money learned in their families of origin into their own marriage. Another became angry and frightened about a violent patient and recorded his automatic thoughts realizing how truly "automatic" they were. Another reported that upon the birth of his second child he became intensely anxious about his elderly father, who was living in another country. The diary helped him see a connection between these feelings and the death of his mother on his first child's birthday.

Discussion of such issues will encourage trainees to look further for underlying schemas in their own lives. One trainee became intensely angry when patients did not inform him of their decisions to change medication, or when administrators did not treat patients correctly. His excessive anger was associated with a sense that he was "being ignored." The trainees in the group related that to his "need for control," and possibly to his fear of "being abandoned." The trainee accepted the first idea but denied the relevance of the second. He began to see the outline of his conflict and underlying distorted schema.

They began to discover that people rarely change when humiliated. They are more likely to change when viewed positively and respectfully.

## Session 5

Purpose: To review two videotape vignettes excerpted from therapy sessions with Dr. Beitman. Direct trainees to use the second-level patterns associated with the several schools of psychotherapy to define "well-formed" patterns.

**1.** The group members watch segments of Beitman's sessions with MC and MF and discuss the patients' patterns.

Before the group watches the tape, present the following information about the patients: MC is a "Southern Belle" with generalized anxiety disorder, treated with low doses of Effexor. She has trouble saying "No." (This session is also used in Module 5 as a demonstration of interpersonal strategies for change.) MF is a 48-year-old woman with panic disorder and an odd form of agoraphobia. Rather than being confined to her house, she must periodically leave because of high anxiety. The segment describes her struggles with her husband and her fear of expressing her needs to him. (This third session from MF was used as a transcript in Module 2 and as a videotape to be rated for working alliance in Module 3.) You may use tapes of your own faculty in session that illustrate problematic patterns being defined during therapy.

Trainees are asked to describe the patients' patterns. They should be encouraged to clarify specific inducing points. Most trainees can filter information on their own and identify patients' patterns. They tend to describe general patterns, such as "the patient has low self-esteem." Encourage them to refine those patterns until they develop suggestions about how to change.

**2.** Trainees struggle with the complexity of the association between fear, anger, and anxiety. They are able to try different theoretical formulas for packaging the pattern. For the vignette with MC, most trainees can identify with her need to please, and can generate several alternative descriptions of the pattern using past-present, automatic thoughts, interpersonal schemas, and so on. The discussion usually yields some interesting questions about how therapists make value judgments based on underlying cultural assumptions about normal and abnormal behavior.

**3.** Homework: Ask trainees to complete Form 11–2 (Inductive Reasoning to Determine Patterns).

## Session 6 (Optional)

Because it requires careful assimilation of information to perceive patterns from videotape excerpts, you may wish to provide an additional videotape presentation for discussion. Our experience has been that trainees learn well from videotape analysis. If your site has made its own videotapes addressing the skills we are teaching here, you may certainly include them to provide your trainees with additional exposure.

## Session 7

Purpose: To review Form 11–2 case vignettes from which trainees have induced patterns. Form 15–2 is similar to Form 11–1. We repeat this exercise format to help solidify trainees' knowledge base.

**1.** You can use answers to Form 11–2 to facilitate the discussion, which should involve trainees interacting, questioning, and responding to one another, more than with Form 11–1.

**2.** You may notice the differences between trainees' answers to Form 11–1 and Form 11–2. We have seen our trainees' experience some remarkable transformations. Suddenly they can see the possibility of patterns with more texture and complexity than simple *DSM-IV* diagnoses. Their minds are open to ideas from different schools, not only in the case vignettes but in their own working environment.

**3.** Homework: Ask trainees to complete Form 12–2 (Transcripts for Inductive Reasoning) and Form 12–3 (Therapeutic Reasoning by Data Point and Category).

## Session 8

Purpose: To have trainees complete Guided Inquiry (Post-Module 4a) and COSE (Post-Module 4b) during the first 20 minutes, to review Form 14–2 for patterns to be found in two different transcripts, and discuss Form 12–3. You should complete GITC after this session.

**1.** After trainees complete COSE and GI, the group discusses Form 14–2, which follows the same format as Form 12–1. You can use answers to Form 12–2 to facilitate the discussion.

**2.** The first transcript, of a patient treated by Albert Ellis, can lead to a discussion of freedom and responsibility, as well as clarification of differences between cognitive schema and automatic thoughts. How much did the patient's growing up and leaving home influence the course of her father's alcoholism?

The second transcript shows a borderline/narcissistic patient interacting with the therapist. It stirs up countertransference and permits discussion of weak self/other boundaries, grandiose and depreciated self.

Therapeutic reasoning: A few of the trainees could not at first grasp the idea of parallels between past and present. "What happened with her mother, happened with her mother. The boyfriend was entirely different." They moved to a discussion of psychopathology in general. People with psychiatric problems generally tend to repeat the same dysfunctional behavior. They are not resilient. They do not change with new experience by applying old ideas in new ways to new situations. They keep doing the same thing. One trainee suggested the term "fixed action pattern" to suggest how rigidly the pattern is embedded in their behavioral repertoires. They speculated about basal ganglia behavioral scripts that automatically kick into action.

Then they began to see that it was not so much parallels but the same pattern being delivered in similar circumstances. What was the similarity? First, they had to describe the primary childhood pattern with some precision: When the daughter saw the mother leaving to meet another man she began to feel abandoned. Then she became angry, and then she started fighting.

The only difference with her boyfriend was that he was going to meet his car. A big difference to be sure, but he loved his car. When he left to work on it, she felt abandoned. The abandoned feeling was tied to anger, which led to fighting.

**3.** Homework: Ask trainees to preview Module 5 text in *Learning Psychotherapy, Second Edition*.

# SUGGESTED ANSWERS TO FORM 11–1

## Inductive Reasoning to Determine Patterns

1. She cannot accept anything positive about herself. (*Disqualifying the positive*)
   She does not trust men.
2. He held himself responsible for problems he did not create. (*Personalizing*)
3. She gives "love" and she wants to be appreciated, but she cannot ask directly. (*Sacrifices herself in order to obtain the love of others*)
4. She is afraid of somebody criticizing her for not being enthusiastic and warm. (*Overly dependent on the opinion of others*)
   She fears losing friends. (*Fear of isolation*)
5. He tries to avoid the fights by agreeing with her. He is afraid of confronting the marital problems. (*Avoid interpersonal conflicts*)
   He thought quarreling with his wife would lead to losing her. (*Fear of low probability events*)
6. He needed to control his wife; he felt threatened if he could not. (*If someone disagrees with him, he feels threatened*)
7. No matter how hard she tries, she believes she will never do the task right. (*She cannot live up to her own expectations and believes others hold her to the same very high standards*)
8. The patient arbitrarily concluded that people will not negotiate with him. (*Jumping to conclusions*)
9. Her pattern: blame him entirely for events to which she partially contributed. (*Blame others, do not accept blame*)
   His pattern: to accept the blame entirely without insisting that they both contributed. (*"Everything bad is my fault."*)
   The couple patterns: she blames him for all problems between them; he accepts the blame. (*One takes too much responsibility, the other takes too little*)
10. She feared that she was not competent anymore because of the brain injury, and that her colleagues would find out and she would lose her job. (*Excessive fear of failure based upon a real possibility*)
11. Similar to the way she reacted to the death of her dog. She became acutely anxious and distressed. (*Exquisitely sensitive to interpersonal loss*)
12. No matter how hard she tries, no one will care about her. Those who clearly do not care about her can become objects of hate. (*Terrified by and furious at those who abandon her*)

# SUGGESTED ANSWERS TO FORM 12–1

## Transcripts for Inductive Reasoning

*Case 1:*

### The patient's possible patterns:

1. She perceives things with "all or nothing" or "white or black" attitude.
2. She can't accept positive or good feelings about herself.
3. She anticipates the bad feeling after the good feeling.
4. She believes other people can be helped, but not her.
5. She can't maintain a relationship with a man, but she needs a man to be happy.
6. She is content when in a relationship with man, but feels depression when by herself.
7. When a relationship goes well, you expect it to go bad.

*Case 2.*

### Rachel's possible patterns:

1. She behaves like a boy to please her father, and tries to comfort him.
2. She thinks she is the one who takes care of and comforts her father in this family.
3. She takes too much responsibility for her father.

### Mother's possible patterns:

1. When she feels lonely or needs somebody to be nice to her, she will go back to her parents.
2. Nobody except Sandy in this family really takes care of me.
3. I go back to my parents because they are old and need me.
4. She thinks her husband needs Rachel to take care of him rather than a wife.
5. She feels rejected by the rest of the family and allows Rachel to take over caring for her husband.

### Father's possible patterns:

1. He complains of his wife being too close to her family.
2. He pays more attention to Rachel than to his wife.
3. The fact that he is not in the interview may be significant. He may be content with the current situation.

### Possible patterns between Rachel and her father:

1. Rachel tries to please him by being like a boy, but she is not successful enough.
2. Rachel plays two roles with her father: One is father's boy, the other is a nurturing pseudo wife.
3. Father likes Rachel's boy personality and becomes accustomed to her caring about him.

### Possible patterns between Rachel and her mother:

1. Rachel doesn't believe her mother can take care of her father.
2. Mother doesn't like her daughter's boyish characteristics.

**Possible patterns between the mother and father:**

1. She blames him for not taking care of her.
2. He blames her for choosing her parents over him.

**Possible patterns among Rachel, father, and mother:**

1. Mother complains that her husband doesn't care about her and doesn't need a wife because he pays more attention to Rachel than to her. Rachel can take care of her father as a daughter and please him by acting like a boy. By going back to her parents for comfort rather than turning to her husband, mother allows Rachel and her father to maintain their alliance.

## SUGGESTED ANSWERS TO FORM 11–2
### Inductive Reasoning to Determine Patterns

1. She could not accept that her mother treated both of them equally. (*Disqualifying the positive*)
2. He preferred to tough it out rather than correct the difficulties. (*Persistently avoids confronting difficulties*)
3. It is hard for her to say "No" to somebody else's requests. (*Other people's needs and wishes are more important than her own*)
4. She must feel superior to other women or else she cannot develop a relationship with them. (*Win or leave*)
5. If things are not just as they should be, he is a failure. (*Tyranny of the "shoulds"*)
6. She thinks that nothing could help, no matter what she does. (*Lack of belief in her own ability to effect a better future*)
7. He abuses her with his drinking. He becomes sober and apologizes when she threatens to leave. She does not leave. (*Whatever he does, she accepts*)
8. People in authority over her will ignore her needs. (*No one cares about me*)
9. She inhibited herself from any sexually suggestive conduct with a man because the man might think she was promiscuous and would leave her. (*Excessive sense of influence over the behavior of others*)
10. If the person with whom he is involved withdraws emotionally, he feels threatened with possible abandonment. (*Excessive fear of abandonment by person for whom he cares*)
11. She expects her roommates to anticipate her needs and respond to them whenever she wants. (*Wants others to take care of her needs without having to ask*)

## SUGGESTED ANSWERS TO FORM 12–2

### Transcripts of Inductive Reasoning

*Case 1:*

1. If she doesn't do what her parents ask her to do, she will feel guilty.
2. It is wrong if she thinks of herself.
3. Everything her parents say is right, and she hasn't been able to stop believing this.
4. She fears being rejected by other people, which might relate to the fear of being rejected by her parents.
5. She can't write fiction because she fears that she couldn't do it very well; her family insisted that she couldn't do well in school.
6. She is promiscuous because she thinks this is the only way to be valued, loved, and approved of by a man.
7. Summary statements of problem patterns: "Whatever I do will not work out successfully; I am better off not trying to do well at school, work, or relationships. (I therefore must stay home with my parents and do as they say. If I am successful and leave home, I will feel guilty about my parents.)"
   Restated: "Since I cannot be successful in the world, I must stay home and take care of my parents who need me. I feel guilty for having had thoughts of leaving."

*Case 2:*

1. She blames her husband and refuses to take responsibility for their marital difficulties.
2. Her feelings of self-worth depend on her husband's (or other persons') reactions to her.
3. She feels both entitled and worthless.
4. The simultaneous existence of entitled, powerful, demanding character features and helpless and worthless character features.

# Strategies for Change

## SESSIONS

### Session 1

Purpose: To review text of Module 5 in *Learning Psychotherapy, Second Edition*. This presents the complexities of the process of change, emphasizing the basic sequence of identifying a pattern, giving it up, initiating a new pattern, and maintaining it. Trainees are offered a list of generic change processes (Appendix II) and a longer list of change processes associated with the different schools of psychotherapy (Appendix III). Here they become acquainted with major approaches to helping people change in a highly condensed presentation.

**1.** Review the Module 5 text with the group. There are many details to trigger discussion. The most complicated elements involve the two figures, the table, and the two glossaries. It will require two sessions to complete the text. We suggest that the discussion in this session focus on the three substages of change, three orders of change, generic strategies for change, and the interaction of ECBIS as implied in Figure 4–2. The next session is used to discuss ECBIS strategies for change.

**2.** There is a very strong connection between Modules 4 and 5. The discussion of patients' patterns in the previous module prepares trainees to learn the strategies and techniques. Trainees are also excited to embark upon this module because they anticipate that it will provide them the tools for psychotherapy.

In their various ways, trainees begin to grasp details of the change process. Seeing psychological and emotional change as less mysterious, as well as partially beyond their influence, they become clearer about the process and more humble about their contribution.

**3.** Homework: Ask trainees to read Appendix II (Generic strategies and techniques) and Appendix III (ECBIS strategies and techniques).

## Session 2

Purpose: To further discuss the text and review the ECBIS glossary.

**1.** Appendix III describes the strategies listed in Table 4–1. The group should go review them together. Start by asking some questions about these readings. The discussion will focus on strategies that trainees have trouble understanding.

**2.** Trainees are exposed to approaches from a variety of psychotherapy schools. We try at once to increase their comfort level with ones they already use and to broaden their range of choices. It is valuable for trainees to become aware of how they differ from one another in their predispositions toward the various approaches.

**3.** Homework: Spend about five minutes demonstrating how to complete Form 14–1 (Transcripts for Change Strategies).

## Session 3

Purpose: To review Form 14–1. As they attempt to recognize the strategies used in transcripts, trainees have to go back to the ECBIS glossary and carefully consider the meaning of various strategies and techniques. Form 14–1 also provides a view of how these strategies are used by different psychotherapists.

**1.** The group members discuss Form 14–1, reporting their answers. Focus on the substage(s) of change as well as generic and specific strategies and techniques. You should also provide guidance about the ECBIS strategies and techniques that appear in that transcript, while recognizing that many of the labels for strategies and techniques overlap. While doing this, help trainees to become aware of the relationships between change substages, between the generic and specific strategies, and among the ECBIS strategies and techniques. Use answers to Form 14–1 to facilitate your discussion.

It may not be possible to discuss all ten transcripts in an hour. We have found that psychotherapy supervisors perform two key functions for Modules 4 and 5: (1) go over the definitions in the glossaries and (2) review trainee answers to the homework not discussed.

**2.** Generally, the discussion helps trainees identify, clarify, and discriminate among some confusing strategies.

From the first transcript of Minuchin's case, our trainees see how changes in a father might promote change in a daughter and mother (systems thinking), and how this system orientation differs from an intrapsychic one. Discussion of Greenberg's second transcript will promote understanding of empathic reflections, and how they can influence changes in thinking by focusing on emotion. Basch's third transcript stimulates discussion of the substages of change. Trainees have difficulty seeing that change has taken place, or how this session is helping to maintain it. Instead, they tend to believe that this session is initiating change where none has occurred before.

Some trainees study the glossaries enthusiastically because they believe that they are the keys to conducting psychotherapy. While they generally recognize the value of the previous modules, they find these strategies and techniques particularly appealing for their usefulness.

**3.** Homework: Ask trainees to complete Form 15–1 (Case Vignettes for Change Strategies). Spend about ten minutes discussing the example in Form 15–1, where trainees are asked to consider which strategies or techniques the therapist might use.

## Session 4

Purpose: To review Form 15–1. This homework gives trainees an opportunity to try out the various strategies in a group discussion. The exercise intends to broaden trainees' thinking and choices in dealing with any given patient.

**1.** Trainees are asked to report generic and ECBIS strategies for each case. Answers to Form 15–1 may help you to facilitate the discussion. You can start with generic strategies and then move on to ECBIS strategies. Encourage trainees to try to think about "how to help this particular patient from a variety of approaches," rather than to determine which individual strategy best fits the patient.

**2.** Trainees' answers often reflect their personal orientations. They can widen their choice of strategies by listening to how other trainees justify their selections.

Trainees find these two cases quite time-consuming, because there is much to review and to consider. The first case involves a young woman who wants to be taken care of by her roommates and her therapist. They find it easier than the second, which involves a teacher with a brain injury after an auto accident. They do not know how to deal with her injury—how significant is it and how much is she exaggerating her disability? Instead of inquiring about evidence to substantiate answers to this question, some trainees simply assume that she is brain-injured and should consider retirement.

## Session 5

Purpose: To review and discuss brief videotape vignettes demonstrating strategies focusing on emotion (E), cognition (C), behavior (B), interpersonal schemas (I), and systems (S). These tapes give trainees an opportunity to discuss ECBIS techniques as well as to see other therapists in action: Videotaped therapy sessions give trainees various models to "try on" for themselves.

We suggest that you use two sessions to review these vignettes. [*] Generally, we review E, C, and B in Session 5 and I and S in Session 6. While each vignette could be discussed in greater detail, our purpose here is to seed trainees with visual-experiential images of ECBIS categories.

**1.** Before the group watches each vignette, ask trainees to read its short introduction in *Learning Psychotherapy, Second Edition*. Remind trainees to pay attention to the underlined strategies and techniques. Direct the discussion to focus on the substages of changes, comparing ECBIS strategies, emphasizing the similarity and differences of ECBIS strategies, and helping trainees clarify the strategies as specifically as possible.

**2.** Trainees appreciate seeing the direct application of what they have read. They are often curious about whether these are actors or real patients. (The answer depends-upon which vignettes you have purchased or developed.) They have the most trouble grasping the empty chair technique of gestalt therapy (it is indeed the most complicated). They make interesting comparisons among the therapists, commenting on degrees of support: empathy, encouragement, praise, remembering to ask about the homework you assigned. They note that gestalt therapy stays within the session and that behavior therapy is focused on what goes on outside the session.

---

[*] Videotapes used are Greenberg (1994), Persons (1994), and Kaslow (1994) (order at 1-800-374-2721), as well as Perlmutter and Levine (1992; order at 1-800-532-7637) and Beitman and Yue (1999; order at 1-800-233-4830).

## Session 6

Purpose: To review interpersonal and system videotapes vignettes.

**1.** The procedure is the same as in the previous session.

To help trainers with this module, below are the approximate times at which each of the relevant vignettes starts on each videotape (from the beginning of the tape) and the approximate length of time the vignette should last (of course, you can always show more of the tape!):

E: Dr. Greenberg:     starts at 21:28, lasts for approx. 7 min.
C: Dr. Morris:        starts at 20:14, lasts for approx. 8 min.
B: Dr. Persons:       starts at 2:00, lasts for approx. 8 min.
I:  Dr. Beitman:       starts at 54:55, lasts for approx. 8 min.
S: Dr. Kaslow:        starts at 43:48, lasts for approx. 7 min. (until end of session).

**2.** In our training program, the discussion usually centers around the following questions: Should this vignette have been categorized as interpersonal or cognitive or behavioral? What is the difference between behavioral role-playing and emotion-focused empty chair? How does systems thinking build upon the interpersonal model, which builds upon cognitive-emotional-behavioral models?

**3.** Homework: Ask trainees to complete Form 14–2 (Transcripts for Change Strategies).

## Session 7

Purpose: To review Form 14–2, which has a format similar to Form 14–1.

**1.** The procedure is the same as Session 3. You can use answers to Form 14–2 to facilitate the discussion.

**2.** Trainees continue to struggle with the relationships between and among these five ways of conceptualizing psychological functioning. They begin to see that emotion, cognition, and behavior make up the interpersonal and that the interpersonal makes up systems. They begin to realize that changes in cognition can influence interpersonal relationships, that changes in interpersonal relationships can influence systems, and that changes in systems can influence changes in behavior.

**3.** Homework: Ask trainees to complete Form 15–2 (Case Vignettes for Change Strategies).

## Session 8

Purpose: To have trainees complete GI and COSE (the first 20 minutes), and to review Form 15–2 (the remaining 40 minutes). Complete GITC after the session.

After trainees complete GI (Post-Module 5a) and COSE (Post-Module 5b), they discuss Form 15–2. The procedure for this session is same as Session 4. Use answers to Form 15–2 to facilitate the discussion.

Homework: Ask trainees to preview Module 6 text in *Learning Psychotherapy, Second Edition.*

# ANSWERS TO FORM 14–1

## Transcripts for Change Strategies

| | | | |
|---|---|---|---|
| I | 1. a | 2. d | |
| II | 1. b | 2. c | |
| III | 1. d | 2. c | 3. c |
| IV | 1. a | 2. b | |
| V | 1. b | 2. a | 3. a |
| VI | 1. a | 2. d | 3. b |
| VII | 1. d | 2. d | |
| VIII | 1. b | 2. a | |

# SUGGESTED ANSWERS TO FORM 15–1

## Case Vignettes for Change Strategies

### Case 1

1. The generic strategies and techniques the therapist might use:
   - Define the dysfunctional pattern
   - Decide what to change
   - Take responsibility (such as the responsibility for taking care of herself and the responsibility for change)
   - Self-disclosure (the therapist can help the patient understand why her roommates left her by talking about his own feelings or reactions to the patient's behaviors toward him)
   - Separate past from present (for example, the patient's interpersonal scripts may reflect the patterns with her parents)
2. The ECBIS strategies and techniques might be:

## E:

### Evoking the emotion in the session:

a. Enactment of the patient's feeling when her roommates did not "take care of her" while she was sick.
b. Help her reexperience the feared reactions when others did not respond to her in a way she needed.

### Restructuring emotional schemas:

a. Help the patient access new information through emotional awareness and detailed reexperiencing of illness and being ignored by roommates.
b. Reconceptualize the patient's internal experience by defining more appropriate emotional responses.
c. Confront feared emotion of being abandoned, neglected.

### Maintaining the reorganized emotional schemas:

The therapist can reinforce the patient's new emotional reaction to the same situation.

## C:

### Identifying and challenging the distorted beliefs:

The therapist helps the patient define the distorted belief that "nobody cared about me" by reality-testing and questioning the evidence.

### Creating adaptive and reasonable beliefs:

The therapist challenges the patient's distorted belief by reattribution, developing alternatives, and disputing irrational thinking.

### Repeating and practicing the modified belief in a variety of situations:

The therapist continues to discuss the patient's new thinking when she is in related situations and reinforces these new thoughts.

## B:

### Identifying maladaptive behaviors:

a. Inability to identify situations in which she needs help and to ask others for it: keep a diary for situations in which help might be necessary.
b. Excessive desire to request help from the therapist.

### Change behavior directly:

a. Practice assertiveness with the therapist acting in the role of a roommate.
b. Make small requests of roommate that are not as emotionally laden.
c. Play the role of the therapist while the therapist plays the patient asking for excessive assistance.

### Practice the modified behaviors in various situations:

a. Watch other assertive people as they make requests of others.
b. Practice assertiveness with family members and others in social circle.

## I:

### Identifying maladaptive interpersonal schemas:

a. Analyze the patient's scenarios by demonstrating how the patient repeats with the therapist patterns from her relationship with her roommates.
b. Examine the patient's interpersonal influence by being both a participant and observer (the therapist can help the patient understand others' reaction to her by discussing her influence in the here-and-now relationship; the therapist is likely to be "pulled" to rescue the patient).

### Modifying and altering interpersonal scripts:

a. Provide new and constructive interpersonal experiences by using the here-and-now therapeutic relationship to show concern without rescuing.
b. Help the patient to rewrite, modify, and correct the assumptions underlying her scenarios (for example, help her become aware that her roommate doesn't have the responsibility for anticipating her needs and responding to them without being asked, and that her roommate's inattentiveness doesn't mean no one cares about her).

### Practice modified roles:

a. Practice and reinforce new interpersonal successes that involve not trying to influence other to do for her what she can do for herself.

## S:

### Identify dysfunctional interactions among system members:

(While the patient presents as an individual, she is part of a social circle including a roommate and the therapist.)

a. Analysis of the sequence of communication suggests that the patient's actions have more effect on those around her than she has considered. She acts and her roommates reject her.

### Changing interactional patterns:

a. The patient sets off predictable responses in others by the ways in which she responds to her own needs. Look for the effects on others and then back on herself to find a place to change the predictable sequence.

b. Act on a link in the sequence to change the system responses.

### Maintain new functional interaction patterns to create a virtuous cycle:

a. If she is able to elicit desired responses from others, she will be able to trust them more easily, feel better about herself, and be able to treat others better, who will, in turn, treat her better.

### Case 2

1. Generic strategies and techniques that might be used:
   - Define dysfunctional patterns related to excessive fear of criticism
   - Challenge dysfunctional beliefs and emotions (like "I am not competent anymore and my colleagues will find out.")
   - Decide what to change (quit teaching? more rehabilitation? change thinking?)
   - Face fear of failure (So what if I fail?)
   - Role play herself and other teachers' reactions to her
2. ECBIS strategies and techniques that might be used:

# E:

### Evoking her fear of criticism by role-playing to activate her fears:

a. Help the patient reconceptualize internal experience by role-playing fear of failure and criticism.

### Restructuring her emotional schema:

b. Confront thoughts and relationship consequences of losing her job.

# C:

### Identifying and challenging her dysfunctional belief (she is not competent anymore):

a. Question the evidence for her incompetence after the brain injury. It is entirely possible that the patient felt incompetent in response to excessive fear rather than brain injury.

b. Test reality (Do her colleagues find her incompetent? How bad must she be to lose her job?)

### Creating reasonable belief by allowing new information to enter information–processing:

a. Develop alternatives (help the patient think about other possible explanations for her "incompetence").

   b. Fantasize consequences (what will happen if her colleagues discover that she is now incompetent?).

   c. Dispute irrational beliefs that she is incompetent.

**Practice:**

a. Change self-talk (e.g., change: "I am not competent anymore and my colleagues will find out and I will lose my job," to: "My incompetent feeling is a product of my excessive fears rather than reality," and "I am still competent to do my job, since I have handled it very well for so many years").

# B:

**Identifying maladaptive behaviors:**

a. Self-monitoring of errors in teaching and lesson planning.

**Changing behavior directly:**

a. Relaxation training for use when the first feelings of anxiety begin.
b. Systematic desensitization (construct and confront a hierarchy of fearful criticism and failure).

**Practice modified behaviors:**

a. Use relaxation training while at work (e.g., with aggravating children in the classroom).
b. Learn to face fears of job loss and other potential failures.

# I:

**Identifying maladaptive interpersonal schemas:**

a. Interpretation: With sufficient information, demonstrate a relationship between current self-doubt and family of origin upbringing.
b. Identify interpersonal patterns within the therapeutic relationship: The patient may suspect that the therapist will criticize her for the way she fills the role of patient (e.g., asking for additional medications).

**Modifying role relationship models and altering interpersonal scripts:**

a. Helping modify assumptions underlying interpersonal scripts. She may believe "If I am not competent as a teacher, no one will like me and I will not like myself," or "I am now handicapped. I dislike anyone who does not do her job, so no one really wants to work with me or support me."

**Practice modified roles and patterns:**

a. Draw reinforcement from new interpersonal successes: The therapist can interpret the meaning of positive change—"You have worked hard to demonstrate to yourself that you are competent. You are selecting the positive evidence and you can keep doing that."

# S:

Spouse and family data not given.

## ANSWERS TO FORM 14–2

### Transcripts for Change Strategies

|      |       |       |
|------|-------|-------|
| I    | 1. a  | 2. a  |
| II   | 1. d  | 2. d  |
| III  | 1. a  | 2. a  |
| IV   | 1. b  | 2. b  |
| V    | 1. c  | 2. a  |
| VI   | 1. c  | 2. a  |
| VII  | 1. b  | 2. b  |
| VIII | 1. a  | 2. d  |
| IX   | 1. c  | 2. c  |

# SUGGESTED ANSWERS TO FORM 15–2

## Case Vignettes For Change Strategies

### Case 1

1. Generic strategies and techniques that should be used with this patient:
   - Defining the dysfunctional pattern (he arbitrarily concludes that people will not negotiate with him—jumping to conclusions)
   - Challenging the dysfunctional belief ("How do you know I would be angry?")
   - Deciding to change his belief that others will not respond to his needs
   - Alter future expectation of people's response to his needs
   - Face fear of bringing up his needs or fear of being refused
   - Practice new assertiveness
2. The ECBIS strategies and techniques for this patient:

# E:

### Evoke emotion in the session:

Evoking the patient's emotion by enacting the real situations (such as talking about the immediate feelings when the patient didn't ask for the more convenient time, or the same feelings in similar situations).

### Restructuring an emotional schema:

a. Helping the patient to access new information through emotional awareness (help the patient to be aware of his irrational fear of being ignored and refused).
b. Reconceptualizing his internal experience by helping him understand his emotional schema.

# C:

### Identifying and challenging his dysfunctional belief:

Questioning the evidence and testing the reality for his dysfunctional belief (for this patient, the therapist questions the evidence for his belief that his demands are always ignored or refused. The therapist tries to help the patient find evidence that some people really care about his needs).

### Creating reasonable belief by introducing new information that is discrepant with the established belief system:

a. Developing alternatives (help the patient find an alternative explanation when people don't negotiate with him).
b. Fantasizing consequences (help the patient imagine what would happen if he were to articulate his needs and people wouldn't negotiate with him).
c. Disputing irrational beliefs: "What do I (the therapist) get out of ignoring your request?"

### Repeat or practice the modified belief:

Change self-talk (The patient might develop self-talk, such as "Since I can't know what other people's reactions will be until I bring up my needs, I won't conclude beforehand that they will neglect my needs." "If people don't want to negotiate with me, they may have reasons that are not necessarily related to me").

## B:

### Defining maladaptive behaviors:

Behavioral observation by the therapist: Note other instances when the patient avoids acting on his own behalf with the therapist.

### Changing behavior directly:

Self-reinforcement: Patient rewards himself when asking for what he needs.

### Practice modified behaviors in various situations:

Keep trying new assertiveness.

## I:

### Identifying maladaptive interpersonal schemas:

Cyclical psychodynamics: Discover that the patient ignores his needs as he induces others to ignore them.

### Modifying role relationship models:

Corrective emotional experiences: The therapist responds graciously to the patient's needs.

### Practice modified roles:

The therapist repeatedly responds graciously to the patient's needs.

## S:

No significant other described.

### Case 2

1. Generic strategies and techniques to be used with this patient:
   - Defining the dysfunctional interactive patterns in this couple
   - Deciding what to change
   - Taking responsibility (especially the wife, take the responsibility for problems between them and the responsibility for changing the pattern between them)
   - Suggesting how to change (the therapist can make several specific suggestions of how to change their reactions to each other)
   - Face fear (especially for the husband, fear of confronting his wife's blame)
   - Practice (practice the new reaction pattern between them)
2. ECBIS strategies and techniques to be used for this patient:

## E:

### Evoking emotion in the session:

Enactment of conflict splits—two chairs: Have him play two parts talking to each other—his inflexible, self-punishing, restrictive self addresses his hidden, angry, resentful self, asking: "What makes you so rigid?"

### Restructuring emotional schemas:

Confronting feared emotions: Help him experience his fear of being assertive.

## C:

### Identifying and challenging dysfunctional beliefs:

Understanding idiosyncratic meaning: For this patient, taking responsibility means being responsible for anything that goes wrong.

### Creating adaptive and reasonable beliefs:

Listing positives and negatives of change: List consequences of insisting that his wife be more responsible for what happens between them (e.g., divorce vs. a more loving relationship).

## B:

### Defining maladaptive behavior:

Self-monitoring: List all instances in which the wife blames him for problems at least partially of her own making.

### Changing behavior directly:

Assertion training: Learn how to identify and dispute the wife's excessive blame.

## I:

### Identify maladaptive interpersonal schemas:

The therapist helps the patient to become aware of his pattern of always accepting his wife's blame and never challenging and confronting her accusations. If his wife joins the therapy, promote awareness of her dysfunctional pattern of blaming the husband rather than sharing or accepting personal responsibility for problems.

### Modify role relationship models and alter interpersonal scripts:

Their interpersonal role disputes involve proper distribution of responsibility.

## S:

### Identifying the dysfunctional dynamic interactions between the spouses:

a. Circular questioning.
b. Enactment of real interactive situations in the session.

### Changing interaction patterns:

a. Creating new structures by altering interactions.
b. Task-setting between the spouses.

### Maintaining the new interactive pattern

Initiate and maintain a virtuous cycle (e.g., less blaming by the wife, leads to more confidence in the husband, leads to less blaming).

# *Resistance*

## SESSIONS

### Session 1

Purpose: To review the text of Module 6 in *Learning Psychotherapy, Second Edition*. Here trainees discover the common but often overlooked tendency of people to resist doing what is in their own best interest.

**1.** The discussion will concentrate on the concept of resistance—its sources, forms, and management. The four tables in the text provide a good summary of the content.

**2.** Trainees recall examples of resistance in their own clinical experiences and are likely to bring up these cases. The labels and sources help them to define resistance more readily than before. The discussion of sources also broadens trainees' thinking in analyzing the resistance. Generally, trainees start to become aware that exploring resistance also requires that they examine themselves (i.e., does my inappropriate technique, or my own countertransference, contribute to the patient's resistance?). They also encounter the idea that resistance can provide an "inducing point" for general patterns of dysfunction. For example, a trainee who repeatedly failed to finish her homework was asked if she had trouble completing assignments in other situations. This suggested the possibility that current cases of resistance can reveal key long-standing patterns of thought and behavior.

**3.** Homework: Ask trainees to review Form 16 (Resistance Case Vignettes).

### Session 2

Purpose: To review Form 16. This exercise helps trainees understand and identify signs and sources of resistance, and to think about potential ways to manage it. While discussing Form 16, you can also help your trainees to clarify and reinforce some concepts appearing in the text.

**1.** You can ask one trainee to read each case vignette. Then the trainees report their answers. There are often disagreements among them; you can use those as opportunities to clarify concepts. The group may use Table 6.4 as a reference, and answers to Form 20 can be used to facilitate the discussion.

**2.** Trainees sometimes have difficulty understanding case IV because it challenges them to use the definition of resistance as an impediment to the achievement of a patient's reasonable expectations during therapy. Some trainees have described the source of resistance as "forces from the patient's social network," when the patient is repeating a dysfunctional pattern during the session.

Case V brings out countertransference about "saving the marriage" versus helping an individual change. There is insufficient evidence that the husband is impeding change. He might be, but we don't know. In case VII, a trainee in our program had trouble labeling the reaction as transference because it seemed to her more like prejudice, which she thought of as a "lack of information." The connection between prejudice and transference lies in generalization from a small bit of information to a stereotyped view of another.

**3.** Homework: Ask trainees to complete Form 17 (Resistance Case Vignettes).

## Session 3

Purpose: To have trainees complete GI and COSE (the first 20 minutes) and to review answers to Form 17. These homework assignments help them to clarify the forms, sources, and responses to resistance. You should complete GITC after this session.

**1.** After trainees complete GI (Post-Module 6a) and COSE (Post-Module 6b), they discuss Form 17, reporting their answers and discussing disagreements. Guide the discussion toward the sources, forms, and management of resistance. Ask trainees to answer each question. Note differences between the answers to Form 21 and the trainees' answers. Use vignettes when there are discrepanices for discussion.

**2.** Case II raises questions about the need to systematically expose the person to a feared stimulus. The data suggest only that exposure may occur too soon, but trainees offer many other reasonable possibilities. Case VII raises the question of pessimism about change vs. the pattern being displayed; the data are closer to demonstration of a pattern. All cases emphasize a need to start with the information available. Trainees tended to infer more possibilities than are actually present: "Look at the moss on the tree, not for a whole forest, because we don't know yet if this tree is in a forest or in someone's backyard."

**3.** Homework: Ask trainees to preview the text of Module 7 in *Learning Psychotherapy, Second Edition*, before the next session.

# ANSWERS TO FORM 16

## Resistance Case Vignettes

|      |       |       |
|------|-------|-------|
| I    | 1. d  | 2. c  |
| II   | 1. a  | 2. c  |
| III  | 1. c  | 2. b  |
| IV   | 1. c  | 2. c  |
| V    | 1. b  | 2. c  |
| VI   | 1. c  | 2. b  |
| VII  | 1. d  | 2. c  |

## ANSWERS TO FORM 17

### Resistance Case Vignettes

| | | |
|---|---|---|
| I | 1. c | 2. b |
| II | 1. a | 2. b |
| III | 1. b | 2. d |
| IV | 1. b | 2. b |
| V | 1. b | 2. a |
| VI | 1. b | 2. c |
| VII | 1. c | 2. d |
| VIII | 1. d | |

**7**

# Transference and Countertransference

## SESSIONS

### Session 1

Purpose: To review the text of Module 7 in *Learning Psychotherapy, Second Edition*. It will require two sessions to complete this text. The module's major goals are: (1) to help trainees see the universality of transference distortions, (2) to help them recognize when their reactions to their patients and others become exaggerated or otherwise distorted (3), to examine the sources of these reactions, and (4) to consider alternative responses.

**1.** You can start with questions about trainees' reading of the Module 7 text. Help them to understand the concepts of transference and countertransference and to discriminate their sources.

**2.** Trainees will pose several kinds of questions about transference and countertransference, like, "What is the interactive countertransference?", "If resistance occurs only within the therapy relationship, is that true of transference?", and "What triggers transference?" Ideas emerging from past experiences are stimulated by the therapist. The therapist's "stimulus value" strongly influences the kinds of memories, ideas about relationships, and role relationship models that surface during therapy. For example, a pregnant resident is likely to evoke different role expectations during therapy than a female resident who is not pregnant. One trainee described a therapist who needed to be needed and seemed to use her patients as substitutes for the personal social network she had failed to develop. Therapists are not immune to the failures and mistakes we readily recognize in patients.

Other common questions include: "How can the therapist be empathic without stimulating too much transference (like too much dependence)?" and "How can the therapist be empathic without developing too much countertransference?" Some empathy is necessary to help establish the working alliance. Some therapists cannot prevent themselves from joining the patient's experience—they identify with or become continuously involved with the patient's feeling states. The mature therapist is neither fully empathic nor completely objective, but capable of moving easily between these two perspectives.

**3.** Homework: Ask trainees to review the rest of the text of Module 7.

## Session 2

Purpose: To continue to review the introductory text of Module 7. This session concentrates on the signs of transference and countertransference, nontransferential and noncountertransferential reactions, the use of transference and countertransference, and their management.

**1.** As in the prior session, encourage trainees to ask questions about the reading. The discussion of signs of TX and CTX should focus on helping trainees to recognize them quickly once they occur in psychotherapy. Encourage them to consider distinctions between TX, CTX, and nontransferential and noncountertransferential reactions. We emphasize the importance of the observing self in managing both TX and CTX. This discussion offers another opportunity to activate each trainee's observing self, increase their willingness to self-observe, and improve the observing self's functioning.

**2.** Encourage trainees to find connections between what they have learned in the seminars and what happens in clinical work. In our discussion of countertransference signs, one trainee described excessive pity as a hindrance to being objective. Another described her lack of sympathy for chronic pain patients. Trainees learn that if their responses are excessive or inappropriate to the situation, they must ask "How much of this originates with me and how much from the patient?" CTX may also affect pharmacotherapy management. One trainee group displayed the full continuum of positive to negative feelings toward prescription of benzodiazepines.

Trainees recognize that experience helps them determine whether their reactions are CTX or not. They have yet to learn the limits of their reactions to patients. Excessive sympathy for a 100-year-old man who expressed the fear that, "I do not think I will leave the hospital," paralyzed one trainee until he realized with more experience that he could still empathize but had to establish some objective distance to offer the patient a constructive response.

**3.** Homework: Continue reading the Module 7 text.

## Session 3

Purpose: To teach CCRT methods as a practical technique for trainees to use in analyzing the patient's transference.

**1.** The group studies Form 18 (Standard CCRT Category) and Form 20 (Relationship Episodes). You may need 10 minutes to present the following information about CCRT.

CCRT (Core Conflict Relationship Theme) is a method for evaluating patients' relationship patterns. The basic assumption of CCRT is that any relationship interaction has three components: what the patient wants from another person, how that person reacts, and how the patient reacts to the reaction. Therapists can use these three components to analyze the patient's relationship patterns and transference. Using CCRT, therapists should first define the relationship episodes (RE). The RE can be defined as an explicit narrative about the relationship with others or with oneself. In each RE, a person with whom the patient is interacting is identified. The second step includes identifying the three components—W: wishes, needs and intentions; RO: response from others (including the therapist); RS: response of self—in these relationship episodes. The occurrences of particular categories of W, RO, and RS are counted to achieve a rating. The rater looks for a theme or themes that cross REs and apply to most of them. These themes are used to formulate the CCRT. We are not trying to train new therapists to define the RE, or how to count the frequency; instead, we want them to learn the thought process in CCRT, as well as the response categories, to better understand the components of transference and countertransference. (For more information on CCRT, see Luborsky & Crits-Christoph, 1990.)

We suggest that the group study each response listed in Form 18 and discuss ambiguities first. The group then uses Form 19 to practice ways to apply the response categories in their own words.

**2.** Trainees learn categories of responses from Form 18. Knowing these categories can help them identify the patients' interpersonal patterns more readily. During the discussion of Form 19, trainees struggle to find a vocabulary with which to categorize responses. You may have to encourage them to use their own words to describe the patients' responses, and then go back to Form 18 for the standard categories. Form 23 also demonstrates how to do the homework of Form 20.

Our discussion notes the pervasiveness of basic patterns and the importance of caution in drawing generalizations from a single relationship episode, emphasizing that the psychotherapeutically significant general patterns are revealed most consistently in highly valued relationships.

**3.** Homework: Ask trainees to complete Form 20 (Relationship Episodes).

## Session 4

Purpose: To review Form 20. This form will help trainees learn how to use CCRT to perceive patients' interpersonal patterns, including transference, through relationship episode analysis.

**1.** Trainees are asked to report and discuss their ratings for each relationship episode. You can report the standard answers.

**2.** Trainees cannot be expected to get the "right answers" because they are not fully trained as researchers in rating relationship episodes. The aim is to help them isolate the elements of interpersonal sequences in order to discern a pattern (CCRT).

**3.** Homework: Trainees are asked to read Appendix IV, "Sex, Love and Psychotherapy," and complete Form 21 (Questions about "Sex, Love, and Psychotherapy").

## Session 5

Purpose: To review trainees' reactions to "Sex, Love and Psychotherapy" and discuss Form 21. Form 21 helps trainees recognize the signs and sources of transference and countertransference, and heightens their self-awareness of sexual feelings toward patients.

**1.** Start by asking about trainees' general reactions to the paper, then discuss Form 21.

**2.** Most trainees do not want to believe that such things happen between therapist and patient. Intellectually, they recognize that sexual activity can occur, but they have trouble believing that such intense responses could happen to them. They are surprised to learn how common sexual contact between psychotherapists and patients is. One trainee reported that if such reactions took place, he would be responsible for them. This comment initiated a discussion of how CTX creates an opportunity for therapists to learn about themselves, since he acknowledged that he generally feels overly responsible for other peoples' reactions to him. Other trainees are surprised that discussion of patient/therapist sex is possible, since sexuality is so difficult to discuss in any context.

Trainees want to know when it is appropriate to discuss transference with a patient. It should be discussed when it is directly relevant to the reasons the patient is in therapy.

Trainees have less difficulty acknowledging their excessive desires to nurture and rescue than their sexual feelings and fantasies. We discuss how female therapists might be more susceptible than males to the nurturing countertransference reaction.

Trainees often ask when the therapist should express his countertransference reaction to the patient. Ultimately, the answer depends on what is best for the patient and not the therapist. If the therapist feels a strong personal need to discuss the reaction, supervision or consultation should be sought.

## Session 6

Purpose: To watch the videotape vignettes showing transference and countertransference. We want trainees to note the patient's attempts to elicit responses from the therapist, and the therapist's responses to these efforts.

**1.** There are two vignettes: Dr. Beitman's session with J, and Dr. Beitman's report of his reactions to W. J is an obese woman with panic disorder, major depression, and a history of sexual abuse. She is currently living on welfare in a trailer park with her 12-year-old daughter. This was the twelfth session in a one-year period. W is a married mother of two children, is dysthymic, and has been socially isolated most of her life. Beitman's self-statement was recorded before the seventeenth session.

After the group watches each vignette, direct the discussion to sign(s) of the patient's transference. What is the origin of the transference? Describe the interaction between the therapist and the patient. If you were the therapist, how would you handle the patient's transference in that situation? Does the therapist experience countertransference? What is its source? Can you identify sign(s) of the therapist's countertransference? You may also encourage trainees to talk about their own experience with patients as they are reminded of them by the vignettes.

**2.** The session with J may induce frustration in some trainees. Our discussions have focused on the therapist's countertransference, as evidenced by his tone of voice and body language.

Trainees often have difficulty believing that the discussion of love Beitman reports having with W can happen in psychotherapy. One group was silent for a long time after they watched the tape. They responded that it would be an extremely difficult situation for them to handle if it were to occur in their practice. The group discussed how and why this intense feeling between the therapist and the patient could occur in psychotherapy. One of our trainees shared the countertransference experience she had when a patient told her his fantasy of having sex with her. This trainee's revelation seemed to shake the group's belief that erotic transference and countertransference could not happen to them. One trainee wanted to leave the therapy session whenever patients said, "Tell me what I should do," to her. Several female trainees reported how strongly they want to take care of those patients who remind them of their brothers and sisters.

Watching Beitman's self-statement helps trainees gain awareness of the importance of monitoring their own thoughts and feelings toward patients. Generally, they respond well to Dr. Beitman's willingness to examine his own feelings and appreciate that he is revealing some personal imperfections to improve their learning experience.

**3.** Homework: Ask trainees to complete Form 22 (Analysis of Your Reactions to Other People).

## Session 7

Purpose: To review Form 22, which provides another opportunity for trainees to observe their own interpersonal (not necessarily dysfunctional) patterns. We try to reinforce the observing self by asking them to examine their responses to one significant other and to one patient.

**1.** The discussion of Form 22 challenges trainees to explore their personal feelings. Some trainees may not be ready to share their experiences with the group. You can ask for a volunteer to start. As in group therapy, honesty should be nurtured; it helps trainees to understand one another, to support each other, and to share their feelings and experiences. Guide them toward thinking about the sources of their reactions to each other, and toward the similarities between their reactions to the significant other and to the patient.

**2.** Some trainees may achieve insights through the discussion. We believe this exercise improves trainees' personal growth. It may accomplish the goal of teaching trainees that they all form basic patterns in their intimate personal and professional relationships, helping them to see how these basic personal patterns influence their reactions to patients.

Several trainees in our groups saw parallels between their reactions to patients and their reactions to significant others. In describing reactions to relationships, two trainees saw the similarity between their reactions to their mothers, each of whom was low functioning and toward whom the trainee felt a need to nurture and support. One of them thought it was "silly" that he had not seen the pattern of saving others recurring in his relationship with his mother. It was suggested that *silly* protected him from having to recognize that he may be protecting his mother from his own anger at her.

Another trainee discovered that her reactions to her husband strongly resembled her relationship to one of her brothers "whom I loved a lot and fought with most of the time." She wondered why her relationship had reached this point with him, since it "did not start out this way." One trainee described how he "tried to give his son everything," perhaps because his father was a rigid disciplinarian and gave little. He began to wonder if he was giving too much to his son. The trainee had been overly giving to one of his patients.

**3.** Homework: Ask trainees to complete Form 23 (Transcript of Borderline Patients).

## Session 8

Purpose: To review Form 23. This exercise uses borderline patients to trigger trainees' countertransference reactions, and then helps them to identify, observe, and analyze these reactions. Again, we emphasize the use of the observing self.

**1.** After reading each transcript, trainees answer the questions. For the first question, trainees tend to analyze the patient's problems rather than report their feelings while reading the transcript. Ask them to project themselves into the therapist's role, then to focus on their emotional reactions to the patient and report them. The second question is intended to demonstrate similarities and differences in trainees' reactions to borderline patients. The differences can prompt discussion of the sources of these unique reactions (the third question).

**2.** Case 1, of the suicidal patient, often triggers anxiety and a sense of inadequacy in trainees. They are asked to consider that the sense of inadequacy might also be the experience of the patient (concordant countertransference).

The patient in Case 2 provokes a sense of being devalued, anger (at being devalued), fear (that something bad would happen), and despair (of not helping the patient). Each of these feelings reflects a dominant emotion for each trainee.

Case 3, of the idealizing and then devaluing female patient, is usually more difficult for the men than for the women. Male trainees would have struggled to regain the idealized relationship. Female trainees (when asked to think of the patient as a man) said that they remained objective with most patients, but if a man started to refer to them as "attractive," etc., they might feel quite uncomfortable. The group had trouble seeing that the therapist was not really "bored," but was reacting to the patient's discussion of another man.

**3.** Homework: Ask trainees to complete Form 24 (Case Vignettes of Transference and Countertransference).

## Session 9

Purpose: To review Form 24, the goal of which is to help trainees become familiar with the various types of transference and countertransference. When asked to categorize the types of transference and countertransference, trainees must consider carefully the origins of these responses.

**1.** Trainees are asked to report their answers. You can use answers to Form 24 to facilitate the discussion, which should clarify several types of TX and CTX. You can focus on the cases to which trainees give answers at variance with the standard ones.

**2.** Trainees seem to understand patient-originated and therapist-originated TX or CTX very well, but are often more confused about the interactive one.

**3.** Homework: Ask trainees to complete Form 25 (Transcripts of Transference).

## Session 10

Purpose: To have trainees complete GI (Post-Module 7a) and COSE (Post-Module 7b), and review Form 25. You should complete GITC after this session.

Use the first 20 minutes for trainees to complete GI (Post-Module 7a) and COSE (Post-Module 7b). The remainder of the session is to discuss Form 25, which teaches trainees how to manage patients' transference.

**1.** Form 25 reports an experienced therapist's responses to patients' transference. Ask trainees to imagine themselves as the therapist and to think how they would respond to the patients.

**2.** Trainees formulate various responses to the patient and struggle with finding the "right answer." They should be told that there are no "right answers." Emphasize learning more possibilities, or new ways to respond to patients' transference.

Trainees' responses may reflect their interpersonal patterns. For example, one of our trainees repeatedly used "why," instead of "how," to question the patient.

In our group, we examine the power of the here-and-now discussion of "How I feel about you." Dr. Beitman was able to show them a feeling of heightened awareness using an exercise in which trainees paired off and looked at each other, anticipating how the other might react. Their heart rates accelerated—we might call that anxiety, but what was it?

One resident asked about what, if any, conditions could be suitable for a patient and therapist to be sexually involved. The group concluded that there were *no* conditions making therapist/patient sex permissable.

**3.** Homework: Preview introduction to Module 8 in *Learning Psychotherapy, Second Edition*.

## SUGGESTED ANSWERS TO FORM 19

### Relationship Episodes–Class Practice

*Relationship Episodes from Ms. Smith*

**Session 3**

**RE #3: Brother and his wife**

1. W: To get out of bad relationship (18, 23)
2. RO: Rejecting (4, 14)
   RO: Put down (6, 8)
3. RS: Feel bad about self (26, 17)
4. W: To be in good relationship (3, 2)
5. RS: Feel bad (22, 20)
6. RO: Dishonest (8, 15)
7. RO: Putting her down (8, 14)
8. RS: Anger (21, 6)

**RE #4: Boyfriend**

1. W: To stop bad relationship (18, 23)
2. RO: Rejecting (4, 14)
3. RS: Assertive about stopping, rejecting relationship (11, 14)
4. RO: Stopped talking to me (11, 14)
5. RO: Didn't contact me (12, 4)
6. RS: Anger (21, 6)
7. RS: I stop contact with him (18, 23)
8. RS: anger (21, 6)
9. RS: Reject other (6, 21)
10. W: Not be lonely again (11, 14)
11. RS: Lonely, crying (23?, 22?)
12. RS: Crying, sad (22, 23)
13. W: Not to feel isolated (11, 14?)
14. RS: Isolated (23, 20)
15. RS: Anger (21, 6)
16. RO: Other friend gave support (13, 3)
17. RO: Gave no support (14, 4)
18. RO: Gave no support (4, 14)

**RE #5: Father**

1. RO: Asshole (25?, 4?)
2. RO: Rejecting, nonsupportive (14, 4)
3 and 4. RO: Rejecting, nonsupportive, nonloving (14, 4)
5. RO: Noncaring (14, 4)
6. RS: Awareness of his nature (1?, 6?)
7. W: To get money (13, 8?)
8. RO: Nonsupportive (14?, 4?)
9. W: To get money (13, 8)
10. RS: Shame about her asking for money (26, 25)
11. W: To end nonsupportive relationship (18, 23)
12. RO: Denies he is asshole (8? 2?)
13. RO: he is dishonest (8, 14?)

**RE #6: Boss**

1. RO: Nice people (13?, 9?)
2. RS: Feel lucky (29?, 28?)
3. RO: Together with patient (3?, 5?)
4. RS: It was nice (29, 28?)
5. RO: Supports (13, 18?)
6. RO: Helps even at a sacrifice (13, 11)
7. RO: Concern (13, 3?)
8. W: Wish for concern and caring (13, 11)
9. RO: Concern about my feelings (13, 3?)
10. RO: Giving (13, 3?)
11. RO: Nice lady (11? 1?)
12. RS: Feel blessed (29? 28?)

## SUGGESTED ANSWERS TO FORM 20

### Relationship Episodes–Homework

*From Mr. Howard, Age 20, Session 3*

#### RE #1: Mother

RO: Disagrees with his view (7, 14)
W:  To get sexual information
    (8?, 11?)
W:  To get close to M. (11?, 8)

RO: (past) Explains (11, 13)
RO: Rejects (4, 12)
RS: Frustration (21, 20?)
RS: Shame (26, 25)

#### RE #2: Mother

RO: Disagrees with his view (7, 14)
RO: (past) Closeness (11?, 13?)
W:  To be physically close (11, 8?)

RO: Rejection (4, 12)
RO: Choose someone else instead of
    P. (4, 12)

#### RE #3: Therapist

RS: Unresponsive, distant (8, 16?)
RS: Headache (31? —)
RS: Tense (27? 9?)
RS: Lack of support or help
    (20, 17?)
    Lack of response on his part
    (8, 16?)

RO: No rapport (12, 14?)
RO: No rapport (12, 14?)
RS: Lack of response on his part (8,
    16?)

#### RE #4: Mother

W:  To be close, have affection
    (11, 33)
RS: (past) Closeness, affection
    (30, 5)

RO: Blames (4, 14)
RS: Felt alone (23, 20?)

#### RE #5: Girlfriend

RS: Resentment (21, 20?)
W:  To not suffer loss of relationships
    (11?, 33?)
RO: Cut off relationships (4, 14?)

RS: Fear of wish for attachment (?)
RO: Rejects (4?, 15)
RS: Blames self (25, 17?)

*From Mr. Howard, Age 20, Session 8*

#### RE #1: Therapist

W:  To be close (11, 17?)
RO: Forces me to give up girlfriend
    (24, 17?)

RS: Resentment (21, —)

### Dream A: Trainers

W:  To be close to trainer (therapist?) (11?, 27?)
RO:  Stronger (24, —)

RO:  Rejects (4, 17?)
RS:  Not good enough (17, 20)

### RE #2: Boyfriend

W:  To trust, to share (6, 8)
W:  To be close (11, 4?)

RO:  Could screw me (8, 15)

### Dream B: Store

W:  To be fed (13, 11?)
RO:  Too much ice cream (offered?)

RS:  Sick (31?, ?)

### Dream C: Store owner

W:  To buy something (13?, —)
W:  To expose self (33?, —)
RO:  Shamed by ladies (4, 17)

RO:  Pursued by man (15, 4), stronger (24, —)

### RE #3: Therapist

W:  To have trusting relationship (6, 3)
RO:  Untrustworthy (8, 17?)

RS:  Distrust (6? 19?)
RS:  Self-blame (25, 26)

### RE #4: Father

W:  To get money (13?, 8?)
RO:  Does not give me (14, 4?)

RS:  Distrust (20?, —)

# SUGGESTED ANSWERS TO FORM 24

## Case Vignettes of Transference and Countertransference

1. Patient-originated transference
2. Patient-originated transference; patient-originated countertransference (complementary countertransference)
3. Therapist-originated transference; therapist-originated countertransference
4. Therapist-originated countertransference
5. Therapist-originated countertransference
6. Patient-originated transference; patient-originated countertransference (complementary countertransference)
7. Patient-originated transference; patient-originated countertransference (complementary countertransference)
8. Patient-originated transference
9. Interactive transference; interactive countertransference
10. Patient-originated transference
11. Patient-originated countertransference (concordant countertransference)
12. Therapist-originated countertransference
13. Patient-originated transference; therapist-originated countertransference
14. Therapist-originated transference; therapist-originated countertransference

# *Termination*

## SESSIONS

### Session 1

Purpose: To review the text of Module 8 in *Learning Psychotherapy, Second Edition,* and the common aspects of termination.

**1.** The group reviews the introduction to Module 8. Discuss how the various predictors of premature termination correlate with each other. Review the tables in some detail. Ask for examples of termination and loss. For whom is termination more difficult, the patient or the therapist? Look for cases of difficulty in transitioning a patient from another resident. It may take 2 sessions to review the introduction.

**2.** One resident described a problem in transfer from another resident. The patient had expected to see another person, but because she asked for an earlier appointment she was scheduled with the current resident. She was angry. Was this an inducing point? Here she had requested an earlier appointment but did not get the new person she was expecting. Were there other instances in which she had expected more than what was reasonable in her life? She then demanded Xanax. The resident had not seen that the patient's deviation from expectation could be an induction point for a pattern, however. Instead he felt intimidated by her response. We had some discussion of the difficulty some patients have in terminating a single session. How should therapists handle this problem?

**3.** Homework: Complete Form 26. Review the instructions to Form 26 referring trainees to Table 8–4.

### Session 2

Purpose: To define the various categories of termination and relate them to clinical and personal experiences.

**1.** Continue to discuss the introduction.

**2.** How does one predict which patients will have trouble with termination? The residents found it interesting that, in general, therapists may have more trouble with termination than do patients. One person asked if the stages of grief may be used to understand termination. Yes, some patients (and therapists) deny the problem of termination;

some are angry and/or sad. Some try to negotiate a continuance (letters, email, phone calls), while others accept termination.

What is actually meant by *termination*? Does the patient never see the therapist again? The trainees argued about the therapeutic value of final terminations vs. booster sessions and other reasons for return.

For whom should termination issues be a major theme? For patients who in the past have had trouble saying goodbye to significant other people and who are afraid of future involvement with people because they associate saying goodbye with painful feelings?

**3.** Homework: Trainees complete Form 26. They underline elements of this transcript that reflect common termination themes. These themes are then discussed and related to Table 8–4.

## Session 3

Purpose: To identify the common events of termination through examination of the transcript of a termination session.

**1.** Review homework of Form 26. The Module 8 identifies most of the common events of termination that appear in this dialogue. It may be worthwhile to look at previous sessions of this therapy relationship for other indications of common events during termination.

**2.** We reviewed the possible common events of termination as illustrated in this session. We read the dialogue together, stopping at common events during termination. Additional questions discussed included: 1) why did this therapist emphasize the value of saying goodbye directly? (Directly looking at the other person and saying goodbye seems to help establish the separation more cleanly.) 2) Why did this therapist say that he was not going to miss this patient very much? (Honesty may have its limits, but the therapist was trying to say that he had also managed to separate from her). 3) What about his saying that earlier in his career he might have had more difficulty in helping her? (This statement was very likely to be true. The therapist may also have been saying that he has developed as a therapist through this interaction.)

This patient spent approximately 18 months after termination involved sexually with other women. Subsequently she married a man and became a district manager for a large retail chain of stores. We discussed indications in the transcript that suggested that she might decide to stay away from men.

**3.** Homework: Answer the questions following case vignettes 1–8 in Form 27

## Session 4

Purpose: To discuss case vignettes involving termination.

**1.** Group discusses answers to Form 27.

**2.** We had very little difficulty with most of the answers. Most controversy concerned the use of dreams in psychotherapy as illustrated by question # 7. One male resident reported a dream described during an initial evaluation of a patient for pharmacotherapy: "My husband and my father-in-law were hovering over me, flying over me, in black coats and pants with knives in their hands." How does one interpret dreams? We discussed the necessity of having "two-minds" one that is open to many possibilities, the other that generates hypotheses to be tested. The patient is the primary source of possibilities. Starting with the most emotionally laden subjects is crucial. It is also important to stay away from placing one's own interpretations on the patient until patterns are clear. For example, the patient's dream of the black-clad relatives could have been sexual, but more likely described her fear of the potential assault by the new caregiver. The context of the initial interview suggests the latter, but what does it tell us about her relationships with important men in her life? Another trainee reported a dream related by a patient during the first session often being transferred from his prior therapist. The dream indicated uncertainty about whether her gains would continue with this new therapist. The new therapist responded by saying: With the great work of Dr. X, it will be easy for me to continue to support you." The group wondered whether he had put himself in a position of potential failure by indicating that he would be there to help her no matter what happened. More importantly, he had overlooked her obvious need to explore the loss of her previous therapist.

    **3.** Discussion of answers to vignettes 8–16 in Form 27.

## Session 5

Purpose: To discuss case vignettes involving termination and to add personal clinical experiences.

    **1.** Review the answers to vignettes 8–16 in Form 27.

    **2.** In considering forced termination, the group wanted to know when it was best to force a conclusion to therapy. The data were not clear, and intuition is required to determine which patients are most likely to respond well to a forced termination.

    **3.** Optional Form 28. If this is your last module group.

# ANSWERS TO FORM 26

## Common Events in Termination

Leaders should discuss the phrases in bold. The sign of patient readiness to terminate is in italics (in braces) after each phrase.

M:  (1) [I don't know how to say this, but I've been trying to figure out how to help myself without you, and I realized that I think about what we are going to talk about before I come here, and now **I'm able to put things together myself.** I need to be able to stop and let myself be with myself and think things through and come up with what I need to know. I can put things together myself.] {*Patient doing work without therapist.*}

(2) [You say that it is me that makes the changes, and I say it is you that made them happen. That's all wrong. We did this; **we did this together.**] {*Attempt to ascribe causation to change—resolved by defining collaboration.*}

(3) [I've got a friend, Jason. We work together, and sometimes we sit and talk together. He has a girlfriend to whom he is really committed. And we talk. I'm not trying to get him to like me. I just am able to talk with him and listen to him. He is a man I can trust. **I can see that there are men out there that I can trust.** {*Developing a new trusting relationship. Therapist is trustworthy, so maybe there are other men who could be.*} Am I making sense?]

T:  You are describing things that people who are completing a helpful therapy often describe. You are able to do for yourself what you and I have been doing together. And, you are able to develop a trusting relationship with a man whom you respect.

M:  Last night, I had an experience that is really hard to explain, really hard. Chris had been out of town for a week. He never called me. I didn't like not hearing from him. I knew things were changing with him. Last night I was with Tom. I used to love Tom last year, and in some ways I still do. We had sex. Jason says having quick sex before getting to know someone is the easy way. The harder way is to let them get to know you slowly. I'm getting to think that Jason is right. Before Tom and I had sex, I realized that I did not bring any protection,

(4) [but the big problem before in situations like this is that I did not say anything and just went along and took the big chance. **This time I said something.** {*Change pattern of not speaking up to protect self from getting pregnant.*} And Tom said he had some protection, and he used it. It was good. But afterwards I felt drained, numb inside. I took a hot bath.]

(5) [**And then the threads of my experience began to come together.** I started to cry, to sob, couldn't stop it. I was happy and sad at the same time. Women have been told that the reason they have sex is for the security of being held, for closeness, because they have low self-esteem, and they want some reassurance. I knew that didn't fit for me, but I didn't know how. Then, last night I saw it. All those guys I had sex with were no good. They didn't deserve my love. None of them. I didn't respect them. And the reason I had sex with them was to prove that they didn't deserve my love. They were just there for the sex for me. They didn't deserve what I had to give them. Just like my Dad. He didn't deserve it either. Now I see how men must feel when a woman wants to have more than just sex. They kind of sneer inside and wonder what's going on. They don't respect the

women, they just want to use them for sex and prove that is all they're good for. They don't respect women.] {*Example of developing insight on her own. Connected father to other men and her own motivation for sex.*}

Now I can feel love because there are men out there like Jason and others who I can respect. There are plenty of no-good men and woman out there, but some can be respected.

(6) [My Dad and I are getting along really well. **I can love him despite his faults.** As you said, he didn't love me the way I wanted or I needed, but he loved me some, and I can accept his limitations. {*Accepting limitations of parental love.*} He keeps asking me is there something more I'm hiding from him because we are getting along so well.]

(7) [I talked to Chris this morning, and told him I didn't want to have sex with him anymore. He is like all the other men, too. He is there only for sex with me. I said we are friends who just fool around. But, I don't respect him. He wanted our relationship to go further, but now I don't. He's leaving town in a few months, and I know we are going nowhere. So, I wanted to stop it before it went any further down a dead end.] {*Latent content for saying good-bye to therapist as well as saying good-bye to men who are only with her for sex.*}

(*She pauses and looks at him quizzically.*)

(8) [I feel you are going to say that I'm talking nonsense, and that I need to stay in therapy for a long, long time.] {*Ambivalence about termination.*}

T: That's absurd. Not true. Quite the opposite. We have to look at what makes you say that.

M: I don't know why. Maybe I was trying to get feedback from you.

T: Then you could have asked me directly for feedback. I believe that was one of the multiple meanings in what you said, but not the only one.

M: Here I am again, opening the door for you to tell me what to do.

T: (9) [Not exactly. You are telling me to tell you to stay in therapy for a long time. I know that we both know that you are ready to leave, but **there is a part of you saying something else here.**] {*Therapist attempts to elicit reasons patient may be having difficulty saying good-by. Why does therapist insist that saying good-bye directly is important?*}

M: Well, I think everyone should have a trained person with whom to talk. Sometimes your friends give just awful advice.

T: So everyone should have a therapist forever?

M: Well, no. It is too expensive.

T: This is our last session. Perhaps you are having trouble saying good-bye.

M: Isn't that natural?

T: Of course it is. I am only trying to get you to say it directly.

M: Oh (*she tries to stifle sobs*) . . . . You mean now I have to say the sappy stuff?

T: I think it is there, and it needs to be said, yes.

M: (10) [This has been so important to me. Changed my life. (*She begins to cry.*) You've helped me so much. I feel freed from so much. I knew I could love, but I had so many stumbling blocks in my way; what I put there. I feel like so many of them are removed. **I think I had that experience last night, crying, happy coming together of myself because this is our last meeting.** I was so happy to feel those threads of my life come together.] {*Expression of appreciation, and also, perhaps, how termination can accelerate change for some people.*}

T:   I wonder if there is any more to say.

M:   I hate good-byes.

T:   Why?

M:   They mean something terrible has happened. That's why people say good-bye.

T:   Like . . .

M:   (11) [When I break up with guys. . . my father leaving. What about you? How do you feel about saying good-bye to me?] {*Reminder of past good-byes—most of which were painful.*}

T:   (12) [Oh, now it's my turn. This is a good-bye for me. You have progressed very well and very far. I've learned a good deal from you, including your answer to the question about who is responsible for you changing. Not you alone, not me, but we are responsible. I like learning that answer since no one ever told me that. **I won't miss you very much.** The person who came in here looking for help, needing help, is no longer here. You have matured and can function on your own. **I believe if I would have seen you several years earlier in my career, I would have been more deeply involved with you and not helped you see the separation between us as much.**] {*Therapist expression of reactions to termination—includes progress, responsibility for change.*}

M:   I'm glad I saw you now and not before.

# ANSWERS TO FORM 27
## Case Vignettes for Termination

1. Transfer and then resolve her continuing intense feelings about the suicide.
2. The patient will feel batrayed. The therapist should have discussed the forced termination much earlier and worked on the patient's problems with loss. Transfer might also be discussed.
3. She would be reluctant to let her patient go because her brother did poorly on his own.
4. A gentle "no" might be enough, with some discussion of why.
5. Numbers 1, 2, 4 (#3 might also be useful by paradoxically siding with the resistance).
6. The therapist should not attend. But in this particular case the therapist did attend, and he did so more to meet his needs than the patient's.
7. Dream Interpretation: We want to talk, but other people get in the way. What happened: Rather than discuss the patient's feelings of anger at me about the separation or her sadness over having to lose me, I responded quickly with the suggestion that she could write to me in the new city to which I was going. She was relieved and said, "Now I will know you are out there someplace." We exchanged some letters. I became tired of reading hers and sending mine. I wanted the relationship to end, but I could not bring myself to do it directly. Instead I sent a letter describing how cool the weather was in my new city and littered the pages with other icy references that let her know that I was becoming cold toward her. She never wrote again (Beitman 1987, p. 281–282).
8. The therapist consulted his supervisor because of the strength of his feelings. Since he had never given a patient a gift before, he knew that he was likely experiencing some sort of countertransference. The supervisor helped him to become aware that this was a case of interactive countertransference. The patient had a need to "look up" to the therapist and sought his approval (which he did not get from his parents); he was excessively appreciative of the work they had done. The therapist, who had relatively little experience with such a degree of appreciation from patients, believed that it was especially important to make sure that this patient maintained his gains. He did not want to "let down" this patient. This need to not disappoint the patient was tied to the therapist's own issues surrounding other people's expectations. The supervisor helped the therapist realize that he and the patient were unconsciously colluding to create a relationship that was "special," which might prevent the patient from generalizing his newly-learned skills to other relationships. The therapist decided to discuss this issue with the patient in the few sessions remaining. After openly discussing this issue, the therapist realized that most of his countertransferential feelings were gone, and he felt fine saying goodbye without giving a material gift. The patient, while still expressing a great deal of appreciation, appeared to understand that the relationship was not nearly as unique as he might have built it up to be. They parted on good terms (Mayfield, personal communication, June 1999).

9. Response C. In the actual case, the patient did not respond to comments on his threats. The therapist, fearing the patient's destructive potential, felt required to continue.

10. Response B. Patient-Initiated. The patient repeated with the therapist the kind of relationship she had with her parents when she left home.

11. The letter to the patient said that the therapist was practicing improperly by keeping the patient in therapy for one year. The patient wanted to know if the MCO was correct in this assessment. The therapist hit a stone—or perhaps, a paper—wall. Initially, the MCO insisted that he would have to be approved to be on the panel for each different contract with each different business making a contract with the MCO. Then the MCO insisted that the patient should have been seen for medication management (which had happened, but she refused further pharmacotherapy because of negative side effects), and finally the MCO declared that their decision was final—her therapy was over. The therapist asked to be contacted by the person who made the decision and then turned to deal with the anger, confusion, and sadness of his patient who feared "going it alone" now that the one person she had grown to trust in the world was being taken away. The therapist agreed to see her without charge until she could properly be transferred to an approved provider since she could not afford treatment without insurance coverage. Finally, the medical director of the MCO called to state that they never intended that he should not be able to continue with the case. The medical director refused to explain why the initial letter had been sent (Simon, Grothaus, Durham, Vonkurff, & Pabiniak, 1996).

12. Personal experiences of trainees.

13. In the nursing home, she was required to move about in order to have social relationships. Back at home, however, disability was rewarded with social contact.

14. Remind the patient that she will be transferred, and allow adequate time for the patient to process this change with the current therapist (approximately 6 months). Address any changes in feelings and behaviour that are caused by the knowledge of impending referral. If possible, hold a joint session with both current and future residents (therapists) so that the patient may have some choice in determining her future therapist. As the current therapist, firmly state that even though you will help her with the transition, you will not be able to continue seeing her. Also, reassure the patient of the new therapist's competence and skills.

15. The patient responded by denying his strong emotional reaction to ending the therapeutic relationship. His anger was manifested in missed appointments, refusing to discuss feelings associated with termination in therapy, and premature termination. He believed that he had recovered and asserted his independence to protect himself from feelings of rejection and abandonment.

# *Afterword*

The depth and variety of psychotherapy theories, models, and practices are too great for any volume or training course to address comprehensively. We can best help you to broaden your studies by pointing out specifically what we understand are the limitations of the training program offered here:

1. The method of teaching using limited reading, substantial homework, and seminar discussion has many advantages, but our method does not include more time-consuming and equally valuable approaches, such as case conferences and in-depth reading of classic and practical papers and textbooks.
2. Our approach remains conceptual—practically conceptual, but conceptual nevertheless. We do not attempt in-depth training in generic skills like empathic reflections, relaxation training, or school-specific techniques like interpretation, cognitive restructuring, or role rehearsal. Our program teaches neither how nor when to apply these methods.
3. We have not attempted to articulate a theory of normal human development, a theory of normal personality, a theory of psychopathology, or a comprehensive theory of treatment related to earlier theories. Ideally, but perhaps not necessarily, psychotherapy change models should be related to theories of normal and abnormal development. But we await reports of research findings proving that such a need exists, accompanied by articulation of its theoretical basis.
4. Several areas of content that could be useful to all trainees are not addressed here, but should be prominently considered before the completion of a therapist's education. These subjects include, but are not limited to: assertiveness training, combining pharmacotherapy and psychotherapy, culture and gender issues, as well as integrated approaches to a variety of *DSM-IV* diagnostic categories like major depression, panic disorder, and substance abuse.

This training program can serve as a good introduction to theoretical school-specific approaches. Ideally, the ideas are presented first, followed by training in cognitive therapy, interpersonal therapy, psychodynamic therapy, solution-focused therapies, and/or family therapy. Teachers of these and other approaches tend to believe that particular theoretical orientations are most effective for treating particular problems. While significant research evidence suggests the specific approaches treat specific problems, a broader view suggests that the therapeutic action of cognitive treatment (Lipsey & Wilson, 1993), for example, closely resembles medications like Prozac, Paxil, and Zoloft (Schatzberg & Nemeroff, 1995), because they are effective for a variety of diagnoses. Furthermore, practicing clinicians often combine a variety of approaches to fit the perceived individual needs of their patients (Goldfried & Wolfe, 1996). Few clinicians swear allegiance to only one theoretical approach to therapy, and most routinely combine pharmacotherapy with one or more psychotherapeutic modalities, guided more by the symptomatology of the patient in their care than by dedication to an intellectual construct of mental illness (Beitman & Klerman, 1991). We therefore believe that a sophisticated psychotherapy integration, based upon the foundation presented here, will constitute the future of psychotherapy training and practice.

Finally, we bring you back to the beginning. We believe that psychotherapy training should be an alluring and engaging experience. You learn about yourself while helping others; you study the human condition while serving humanity; you are involved in helping others find their way through life's confusions while resolving some of your own internal misgivings and fears. May fascination and joy be part of your teaching and learning experience.

# Experimental Module 9

# EXPERIMENTAL MODULE 9

## Future-Oriented Formulation

## SESSIONS

### Section 9–1

Purpose: To help trainees grasp how human behavior—their own and that of their patients—is influenced by individuals' conceptions of the future. As a psychotherapy teacher, you will review relationships between expectations and experience, the origins of expectations, expectation videos, self-awareness, the brain and the future, and conceptualizations of the future within the theoretic schools of psychotherapy.

1. Discuss the various ways in which the human behavior is influenced by people's concepts of the future. Use personal examples from trainees' lives as well as from your own recent experience. Include patient expectations and how they influence behavior.

2. Trainees may find that they have trouble switching to a future focus if they rely solely upon models expounded by the various theoretical schools of psychotherapy explain human behavior. Test your own unwillingness to shift into the future perspective.

3. Homework assignments are intended to broaden trainee conceptualizations of the future's influence on behavior.

### Section 9–2

Purpose: Form 9–2 is meant to encourage trainees to conceptualize the movie that is psychotherapy—to learn the variables that predict outcome, so that outcome can be more effectively managed.

1. Discuss the list of therapeutic outcome variables. There may be some missing. Resiliency, for example, may be one such patient variable, or it may be seen as an element of self- awareness.

2. As you review the list, call upon your own experience in changing the experience of your patients, as well as your trainees' experience of personal and professional change. What events could have been seen as predictive of outcome? What variables influenced outcome?

**3.** The homework is intended to encourage trainees to think broadly about the process of psychotherapy, and from this broad perspective to settle into imagining the process with each new patient.

## Section 9–3

Purpose: Form 9–3 is meant to help trainees itemize the variables that influence development of patients' personal futures, notably the patient's own formulation of the problem and what to do about it.

**1.** Discuss each of the sections—especially how the precipitant relates to the developmental challenge, the patient's formulation, and implications for the clinician's diagnostic process.

**2.** Trainees may have difficulty conceptualizing psychotherapeutically while also conceptualizing diagnostically. Diagnosis cuts across groups, while psychotherapy tries to mold itself to the individuality of each therapy patient. Help trainees to understand how developmental challenges play vital roles in mismatches between expectations and experience, in their own lives and in the lives of their patients.

**3.** The homework is intended to be practice for observing the many ways in which futures can be constructed.

## Section 9–4

Purpose: Form 9–4 is intended to help trainees to begin redirecting psychotherapeutic thought toward the more efficient focus of helping patients change how they imagine their futures.

**1.** Actively assist trainees in understanding the meaning of self-awareness, how their observing selves can be activated, and how they can stimulate their patients' self-reflective processes. Use case examples of how the future can be reworked by reassembling memories and experiences into new schemes and scripts.

**2.** Trainees may be wedded to their own views of psychological change. Identify those ways of thinking and try to build on them. Help trainees progress through the basic sequence of finding a problem, activating self-awareness, recognizing the mismatch, and creating new accommodations to reality and expectations.

**3.** The homework is intended to provide opportunities for rehearsing the process of creating new futures.

# ANSWERS TO FORM 9-1

## Fundamentals of a Future Orientation

1. For example:
   I hope that more patients will:
   1. seek their purpose in life.
   2. value the importance of gratitude.
   3. continue to learn about life and serve humanity and all living things.
   4. strive to make their unconscious intentions, plans, and wishes conscious.
   5. study the manner in which we co-create our own realities.
   6. find ways to have fun that also help themselves and others.
   7. find meaningful connections to others.
   8. be resilient in response to difficulties.
2. For example, high self-esteem creates high psychological functioning. (This may not always be true, since people who think they are wonderful are often very self-involved and unwilling to consider the needs of others. High self-esteem based on no accomplishment is contradictory. Some with "low self-esteem" may be humble and appreciative of what they have.
3. Steps include: 1) acknowledge the differences (at least to yourself), 2) attempt to enter into and understand the patient's cultural world view and 3) attempt to work within that world view using culturally sensitive interventions. For example, if the therapist has embraced a feminist perspective and is seeing a Latino man who expects to be the dominant partner, the therapist must then work within this framework.
4. In their traditional culture, they expected respect and obedience from their child. Instead, she grew up in a culture that valued individual autonomy and promoted adolescent rebellion.
5. Steps include: 1) Recognize the form of your reaction (anger, withdrawal, overactivity, criticism, sadness, defensiveness), 2) trace the reaction back to your own experiences and beliefs to attempt to see the specifics of your differences, 3) note that you may have once been part of a culture that supports what you now find difficult in your patient, 4) consistent monitoring of your responses while gaining a fuller appreciation of the patient's need to grow within his or her own cultural milieu.
6. Cultures use fear of death for social control by promising desirable outcomes to those who follow culturally prescribed rules. Examples include: the Greek hero could gain immortality through worthy deeds, otherwise he would be forgotten; Christians could go to heaven if they conformed to Church doctrine; the Hindu could be liberated from physical life and its illusions by controlling his desires; Muslims who died fighting to defend the faith would earn entrance to paradise (Czikszentmihalyi, 1993).
7. Open
8. Open
9. Open

10. Responses:
    a.  Regret: "For of all sad words of tongue or pen
            The saddest are these: 'It might have been!'"
                John Greenleaf Whittier in Maud Muller
    b.  Anger: loss or theoretical loss to self-esteem, property or other perceived possession of the self.
    c.  Guilt: actions of the self-deserving punishments
11. The product of communication is the impact on the listener. The speaker's intent is not necessarily achieved.
12. Sympathy, pity, to undo what he has done to hurt her. An explanation of some kind.
13. Open

# ANSWERS TO FORM 9-2

## Process Variables for Influencing Outcome

1. Personal choice
2. Personal choice
3. Most psychotherapists respond initially with a brief series of answers that include things like *attentiveness, caring, establishing a safe haven, communicating respect, acceptance,* and *empathy.* With a little prodding, most experienced therapists can describe several occasions on which they intentionally violated these supposedly universal conditions. Paradoxical techniques frequently force one to respond unempathically. Confrontations and interpretations may deliberately produce an unsafe feeling. Suspicious and poorly motivated patients may respond poorly to therapists who are particularly empathic, involved, and accepting. To be *attitudinally* empathic is to respond differently to different patients because their past histories, expectations, and role relationship models will vary (Norcross & Beutler, 2000). Professional opinion seems to be gathering around "flexibility" as the most viable universal relationship stance.
4. Not reactant because they wanted to be directed.
5. The patient was perplexed and overwhelmed. Depressed patients often have difficulty making decisions. Also, the one-page handouts had little to do with her problems because they were about forms of therapy and not about her presenting concerns. She canceled the next appointment.
6. I would say "no" because this is not a therapist role (BB).
7. "I stopped sleeping around and cheating on my wife several months ago and will not go back to it" (action or early maintenance stage). "Yes, I recognize my depression and will work to change it" (contemplation stage), "but not my drinking" (precontemplation) (after Norcross & Beutler, 2000).
8. a, c, b, least complex to most complex.
9. A major difference between patient and therapist: patients report experiences that are embarrassing, shameful, and painful. Self-disclosure may reduce that distance but never close it. Self-disclosure may help to show patients that therapists are fallible, ordinary human beings. Determining if this tactic is useful, and if so, how and when to utilize it, will vary among patient-therapist pairs over time (after Maracek, 2001).

## ANSWERS TO FORM 9-3

### Variables Influencing the Creation of Personal Futures

1. Personal
2. Responses:

   A married couple's two-year-old child died from a brain tumor (Future: the couple loses their expectations for a growing, healthy child)

   A 12-year-old girl develops insulin dependent diabetes. (Future: She refuses to believe that she is different from her friends, so she does not follow the diabetic care instructions. Taking care of her diabetes would mean she is different from other teenagers.)

   A 15-year-old son of a religious fundamentalist declares he is gay. (Future: His father anticipates ridicule by his church members and loss of anticipated grandchildren. Not wanting to bear the humiliation or grief, he ships his son to another town.)

   A 21-year-old college student is drinking, smoking much marijuana, and has few friends. (Future: The drugs may have eliminated his ability to plan for the future. He leaves college like a leaf in a stream, ready to be pulled anywhere.)

   A 35-year-old devout Catholic woman has wanted a family and children since he was a young woman. She has no prospects for marriage. (Future: Her desired future is evaporating. How does she replace her old expectations?)

   A 38-year-old law student is living with his parents (Future: Her parents worry about the future of their child when the parents are dead.)

   A 40-year-old woman with three school-aged children and metastatic ovarian cancer (Future: The dying parent worries about the effects her loss will have on their emotional stability. She wonders if they will forget her and how much she loved them.)

   A 49-year-old woman has two husbands die, 15 years apart, each of the same rare bone cancer. (Future: She fears being in another relationship in which her husband will die of bone cancer, which will confirm even further that she is evil and caused the deaths)

   A 65-year-old man is forced to retire (Future: He fears that he will have nothing to do, no one will respect him, and his children will think that he is a failure.)

   A 78-year-old depressed, retired widow (Future: fears of entering a nursing home and being left alone by friends who are dying and relatives who have better things to do.)

3. Precipitants: What expectations have been taken away? For each of the following categories, add two specific examples:

   Role Transitions:
   - geographic move
   - marriage/cohabitation
   - separation/divorce
   - graduation/new job
   - loss of job/retirement
   - loss of physical function
   - financial shift

Role disputes:
- authority/dominance issues
- dependence
- sexual issues
- child-rearing
- getting married/separated
- transgression: lover/spouse emotionally involved with someone else

Unresolved grief:
- loss of a crucial relationship
  of a social role
  of a possession

(after Markowitz & Swartz, 1997, pp. 217–218)

4. Responses:

Dysthymia: Life goes on and on. Put one foot ahead of the other. All I see backwards and forwards in time is bleak, cold and gray.

Major depression: Whatever I do works out badly. No sense in trying. No one likes me or ever will.

Panic disorder: Something bad is going to happen. I know it. I've got to be careful or else I will step into an anxiety trap. Very careful.

PTSD: I can't trust anyone anymore. The world is not safe. I've got to turn off my feelings and avoid going anyplace that might make me feel anything, especially the terror.

Alcohol abuse: I can't feel good any other way. No one understands how alcohol makes me feel. It is my best friend. I am not letting go of the feeling alcohol gives me.

5. I experienced several years of mild paranoia. I understood that paranoid people are often very friendly but just suspicious, and that the best way out of being paranoid was to ask questions about what other people were thinking about me. Collect the facts. Don't just rely on feeling or intuition (BB).

6. When she sees other people with friends like the ones she had in her old town, when she sees a friendly dog like hers, and when she is with her son.

7. Personal: A man has lost his wife after a three year battle with malignant melanoma. One of the MDs who saw her mole before it began to spread told her that there was nothing to worry about. He had two teenage children as did I. My wife's mother and several other relatives had died of breast cancer. What if some lump was missed in her (BB)?

8. To the spouse of depressed patients: it is common for a person in your situation to feel very angry at your husband. What can you do to help?

9. "When people come to you for help, they often do not know what they want from their current investments for their futures and what kinds of risks they are willing to take to get there. You seem to be in a similar position in regard to psychotherapy."

10. These traditional cultures place more value on group membership, respect for elders, and for ancestors. They place less value on individual achievement and individuation.

11. A possible answer heard echoing through the corridors of time: I may be old fashioned but...I believe in fairness and morality. What do you mean by gender equality? After all, I bring home the money. I don't think raising the children is quite equal to what I do, especially now that the children are out of the house.

12. I often ask during the initial interview. Women (and men) have become much more comfortable in talking about these possible histories and usually recognize the significant impact these memories and events can have on current functioning. I try to address the question when the patient appears ready to discuss it within the context of other historical questions (BB).

## ANSWERS TO FORM 9-4

### Future-Oriented Methods for
### Changing Problematic Expectation Videos

1. Example: To a man with a history of panic disorder who had a severe panic attack when he found that he could not handle his new job: Your fear of being out of work, with no one to take care of you and no source of money, terrifies you. An image of being poverty-stricken and alone probably crossed your mind.

2. Among the possible situations: 1) alcoholics who do not want to lose their drinking buddies 2) a parent who does not want to see his/her child leave home 3) a dependent person who does not want to lose a partner.

3. Enjoy the movie!

4. Old patterns are breaking down, making room for new ones to form.

5. The daughter stated, when asked, that because of her strong attachment to her mother, she became promiscuous, began using drugs, and made the suicide attempt in an effort to join her mother in Hell.

6. He was playing out his parents' expectation to fail without them. He also saw himself in a future with weak professional identity and no friends. He would always be different, isolated, and lonely. He also saw a future with positive outcomes based upon his perseverance.

7. The patient responded to the psychiatrist's question about what he wanted, saying, "The only way I can stay off alcohol is if I take Antabuse. I did not get along with my previous psychiatrist and he will not return my calls now. I don't like him. If you can prescribe Antabuse for me, I will probably be able to stay away from drinking and maybe be able to stop my life from falling apart." The countertransference fear and disgust melted with the patient's clearly articulated request. The psychiatrist prescribed Antabuse. The patient successfully stopped drinking and was able to save his job. His wife, nevertheless, decided to leave him.

8. Responses:
   1. Emotionally charged, confiding relationship (reduces isolation).
   2. Rationale and a ritual (a basic theory and specified methods to use the theory) (therapist demonstrates knowledge base and what to do with it–appears competent).
   3. Naming and ordering the confusing experiences of one's life (provides sense of mastery, self-control, and competence).
   4. Providing in-the-office experiences of new knowledge (enhances hope for yet new learning outside the office) (Frank, 1976).

9. By recognizing that all we have is now, that death can happen in the next moment, we can live more fully in the present moment.

   Rather than suppressing death awareness, many philosophies contain suggestions to integrate the knowledge of the temporary nature of human consciousness into one's life so that it will deepen and enrich each experience. Existential philosophers used the phrase "being toward death."

   Yet how are we to conceptualize our places in the universe?

"If it is true that each of us is part of the universal energy pulsing through the vast emptiness of space, if each person's consciousness is due to the momentary combination of (matter and spirit?) flowing through the cosmos . . . . then we need not fear death as the end of existence. . . . . . To figure out how this is true must involve a process of gradual revelations, of endless discoveries evolving through the millennia; an unfolding task in which what we now call science and what we call religion will blend, and then grow into hitherto undreamed of powers of understanding (Czikszentmihalyi, 1993).

10. Responses
    Denial—avoid facing frightening, undesirable expectation.
    Reaction formation—doing the opposite of what one would like to do.
    Splitting—enacting contradicting expectations under different circumstances.
    Sublimation—converting sexual, aggressive drives into more socially acceptable aims.

11. When frightening consequences would lead to failure to act in one's best interest (e.g., Physical activity after a heart attack: could be frightening by increasing heart rate, drawing attention to cardiac functioning, and reminding of potential for repeat infarction).

12. Black/white thinking: limits possible alternatives.
    Personalization: Believing oneself to be the causal element in every event will cause future predictions to be inaccurate and ineffective.
    Minimization: limits ability to predict impact of one's own behavior on environment.

13. Responses :
    - Willingness to believe in the possibility of an improved future and to look for positive opportunities in the midst of negative circumstances.
    - Ability to self-reflect to 1) consider the search for benefit, 2) imagine possible benefits.

14. By challenging mistaken expectations, reality experiences can alter them.

15. Meditation is generally of two types:
    1. Focused – on candle, object – eliminate thoughts of other things.
    2. Mindful – let thoughts come and let them go – allows me to choose what to think.

16. Seminar leader provides personal example.

17. Each of these approaches to life has value under some, but not all, circumstances:
    a. If I make a mistake, the relationship is over.
       "You have learned to be very careful. You have learned to manage the details of relationships mostly ignored by others. Now you can back off from that test of whether or not your relationships will continue."
    b. I better not depend on anyone. I need to only depend on myself. Otherwise I will be let down.
       "You have learned to be independent. Good. You can still rely upon yourself. If you let others in to your life and they disappoint you, you can still rely on yourself and possibly maintain the relationship."

c. I must please everyone, or else I will be rejected.
"You can be popular because you know how to make people smile and like you. Try to be a little less pleasing and a little more true to yourself. See what might happen."

d. I must suppress any expression of vulnerable emotions. Otherwise, it will be used against me.
"You have learned to appear tough; use that toughness when you need to. However, emotionally healthy people don't lock their emotions inside. That makes brittle people, not strong flexible ones. Emotionally healthy people can experience and express a full range of feelings. The challenge now is to figure out when and with whom it is sufficiently safe to experience and express more of your feelings."

18. Refer to Sleep Lab to determine whether he can have erection during REM sleep, since more than 90% of REM sleep is accompanied by penile (and clitoral) engorgement). Consider the possibility that trazodone may be contributing to the problem. Finally, hypothesize that his second wife's surgery reminded him of his first wife's last days. He was again the keeper of the household. How can a man have sex with a "dying" woman? His sense of helplessness, despair, and grief for his first wife was now unconsciously transferred to his relationship with his second wife. He had to separate out the videos of the first from the second, and then construct some new ones.

19. He felt grandiose and depreciated at different times. Sometimes he was the most important person. Sometimes he was the least important person. When grandiose, he expected others to meet his every need. When depreciated, he felt powerless to influence the actions of others. When others did not meet his expectations, he felt slighted and deeply hurt, leading to images of attacking and harming those who hurt him and then feeling guilt accompanied by images of punishment for his excessive anger.

   After years of once-monthly psychotherapy, these counterposing expectation videos became clearer to him, allowing him to dissolve each into the other for more realistic views of himself and others.

20. For example, "re-enactment of past to present" from Psychodynamic theory. This idea clearly illustrates that the "future is remembered", that the past carries us into our ways of acting in the future unless we notice it and decide to change the rerun.

21. For example, "defining dysfunctional patterns" suggests that they be placed aside, removed, altered somehow to be replaced by new scripts for the future.

22. For example, *catharsis* was believed to have removed the "bad feeling" from the psyche by cleaning it out through the expression of intense emotion. However, the schema, script, or pattern containing the emotion does not necessarily change, so the pattern continues to be re-enacted.

# References

Alvarez, A. (1995). *Perceptions of fraudulence, counseling self-efficacy, and satisfaction with work.* Unpublished doctoral dissertation, State University at New York-Albany.

Bandura, A. (1986). (Ed.). *Social foundations of thought and action: A social cognitive theory.* Englewood Cliffs, NJ: Prentice Hall.

Beck, A., Rush, A., Shaw, B., & Emery, G. (1979). *Cognitive therapy of depression.* New York: Guilford.

Beitman, B. D., & Klerman, G. L. (Eds.) (1991). *Integrating pharmacotherapy and psychotherapy.* Washington, DC: American Psychiatric Press, Inc.

Beitman, B. D., & Yue, D. (1999). *Learning Psychotherapy* [video]. New York: Norton.

Binder, J. L., & Strupp, H. H. (1993). Recommendations for improving psychotherapy training based on experiences with manual-guided training and research: An introduction. *Psychotherapy, 30,* 571–572.

Bordin, E. S. (1979). The generalizability of the psychoanalytic concept of the working alliance. *Psychotherapy: Theory, Research and Practice, 16,* 252–260.

Breunlin, D. C., Schwartz, R. C., & Krause, M. S. (1989). The prediction of learning in family therapy training programs. *Journal of Marriage and Family Therapy, 15,* 387–395.

Czikszentmihalyi, M. (1993). *The evolving self.* New York: Harper.

Daniels, J. A. (1997). *The influence of performance feedback and causal attributions upon ratings of counseling self-efficacy.* Unpublished doctoral dissertation, University of Nebraska-Lincoln.

DeGraaf, R. V. (1996). *Counselor self-efficacy development: An examination over time of the influence of trainee exposure to clients' negative affectivity and the supervisory alliance.* Unpublished doctoral dissertation, Loyola University, Chicago.

Dobson, K. S., & Shaw, B. F. (1993). The training of cognitive therapists: What have we learned from treatment manuals? *Psychotherapy, 30,* 573–577.

Frank, J. (1976). *Persuasion and healing.* Baltimore, MD: Johns Hopkins University Press.

Garfield, S. L., & Bergin, A. E. (1971). Personal therapy, outcome and some therapist variables. *Psychotherapy: Theory, Research, and Practice, 8,* 252–253.

Garfield, S. L., & Kartz, R. (1976). Personal therapy for the psychotherapist: Some findings and issues. *Psychotherapy: Theory, Research and Practice, 3,* 188–192.

Goldfried, M. R., & Wolfe, B. E. (1996). Psychotherapy practice and research: Repairing a strained alliance. *American Psychologist, 51,* 1007–1017.

Greenberg, L. S. (1994). *Process experiential psychotherapy* [videotape]. Psychotherapy Video Series I. Washington, DC: American Psychological Association.

Heppner, M. J., & O' Brien, K. M. (1997). Multicultural counselor training students' perceptions of helpful and hindering events. *Counselor Supervision and Training, 34,* 4–18.

Heppner, P. P., & Mintz, L. B. (1997). *An intensive study of the change process in counseling.* Unpublished manuscript.

Heppner, P. P., Rosenberg, J. L., & Hedgespeth, J. (1992). Three methods in measuring the therapeutic process: Clients' and counselors' constructions of the therapeutic process versus actual therapeutic events. *Journal of Counseling Psychology, 39,* 20–31.

Hill, C. E., & O'Brien, K. M. (1999). *Helping skills.* Washington, D.C.: American Psychological Association.

Kaslow, F. W. (1994). *Individual therapy from a family systems perspective* [videotape]. Psychotherapy Video Series I. Washington, DC: American Psychological Association.

Larson, L. M. (1998a). The social cognitive model of counselor training. *The Counseling Psychologist, 26,* 219–273.

Larson, L. M. (1998b). Making it to the show: Four criteria to consider. *The Counseling Psychologist, 26,* 324–341.

Larson, L. M., Cardwell, T., & Majors, M. (1996, August). *Counseling self-efficacy, job satisfaction, and work environment: Predictors of burnout.* Paper presented at the American Psychological Association Convention in Toronto, Canada.

Larson, L. M., & Daniels, J. A. (1998). Review of the counseling self-efficacy literature. *The Counseling Psychologist, 26,* 179–218.

Larson, L. M., Suzuki, L., Gillespie, K., Potenza, M. T., Toulouse, A. L., & Bechtel, M. A. (1992). The development and validation of the counseling self-estimate inventory. *Journal of Counseling Psychology, 39,* 105–120.

Lipsey, M. W., & Wilson, D. B. (1993). The efficacy of psychological, educational, and behavioral treatment: Confirmation from a meta-analysis. *American Psychologist, 48,* 1181–1209.

Luborsky, L. (1993). Recommendations for training therapists based on manuals for psychotherapy research. *Psychotherapy, 30,* 578–580.

Luborsky, L., & Crits-Christoph, P. C. (1990). *Understanding transference.* New York: Basic Books.

Luborsky, L., McLellan, T., Woody, G. E., O'Brien, C., & Auerbach, A. (1985). Therapist success and its determinants. *Archives of General Psychiatry, 42,* 602–611.

Markowitz, J., & Swartz, H. (1997). Case formulation in interpersonal psychotherapy of depression. In T. D. Eells (Ed.), *Handbook of psychotherapy case formulation* (pp. 192–222). New York: Guilford Press.

Perlmutter, A. H., & Levine, T. (producers) (1992). *Psychotherapies* [video]. *The world of abnormal psychology* (vol. 12). Washington, DC: Annenberg/CPB Educational.

Persons, J. B. (1994). *Cognitive-behavior therapy* [videotape]. Psychotherapy Video Series I. Washington, DC: American Psychological Association.

Robertson, M. H. (1995). *Psychotherapy education and training: an integrative perspective.* Madison, CT: International Universities Press.

Sakinofsky, I. (1979). Evaluating the competence of psychotherapists. *Canadian Journal of Psychiatry, 24,* 193–205.

Schatzberg, A. F., & Nemeroff, C. B. (Eds.) (1995). *The American Psychiatric Press textbook of psychopharmacology.* Washington, DC: American Psychiatric Press, Inc.

Sevel, J., Cummings, J. P., & Madrigal, C. (1999). *Social work skills demonstrated: Beginners direct practice CD-ROM with student manual.* Needham Heights, MA: Allyn & Bacon.

Shostrom, E. L. (producer) (1965). *Client center therapy* (Carl Rogers) [video]. *Three Approaches to Psychotherapy* (vol. 1). Corona Del Mar, CA: Psychological and Educational Films.

Simon, G., Grothaus, L., Durham, L., Von Kurff, M., & Pabiniak, C. (1996). Impact of visit co-payments on out-patient mental health utilization by members of a health maintenance organization. *American Journal of Psychiatry, 153,* 331–338.

White, N. K. (1996). *The relationship between counselor-trainee extra-therapy characteristics and success in counselor training.* Unpublished master's thesis, California State University, Chico, CA.